Everyday Chinese Series 1

EVERYDAY CHINESE for TRAVELERS

旅遊中文開口說

Speaking in **Chinese**
Anytime
Anywhere
Anyone

Editor in Chief
Yeh Teh-ming

Written by
Chu Wen-yu, Wang Chiung-shu

The Far East Book Co., Ltd.

PUBLISHED BY

The Far East Book Co., Ltd.

www.fareast.com.tw

North America Distributor

U.S. International Publishing, Inc.

www.usipusa.com

ISBN 957-612-724-6

Using This Book

·*Everyday Chinese for Travelers* is a handy pocket-sized traveler's phrasebook designed for foreign visitors, especially those from Western countries. We collected plenty of dialogues, which are simple and practical, and categorized them according to topic, like accommodations, eating, shopping, etc., making them very convenient to find. Each dialogue is composed of the Chinese characters and their counterparts in pinyin, along with an English translation.

The book also contains a variety of other features. "Word Bank 📖" can help you find related words on a certain topic. "Do You Know? 🔆" gives you cultural information to ease the culture shock. And the "Note 📎" section provides some useful tips on language usage. An essential introduction to pinyin and Chinese grammar is also provided. At the end of this book, we include a Chinese menu, a shopping list, a mini-dictionary and references for tour information to make your stay even more meaningful and enjoyable.

Travelers to Taiwan, Hong Kong, and China will find this book useful for helping you communicate easily with local people without the frustration of learning the language. Trying to use the language is a great way to make friends. However, if you have difficulty making yourself understood, just simply point to the word or sentence you want to say.

Contents

Reservations   39

Transportation   51

Accommodations   89

Eating 111

Tour 129

Hanyu Pinyin

The phonetic symbols used in this book are called "pinyin." Pinyin uses roman letters to represent the sounds of Chinese words. The only challenge you have to face is the tones.

Pinyin can be broken down into 3 major parts: tones, initials, and finals. (To help improve understanding, we sometimes use English pronunciations to represent sounds in Mandarin. However, we strongly suggest you listen to the CD to learn the correct pronunciation.)

In this book, sometimes we choose not to completely obey the rules of the pinyin system, like using diǎr instead of diǎnr. We believe that this should make it easier for you to say the word.

1. Tones: There are 4 basic tones in Mandarin. The tone mark is placed above the main vowel.

1st tone	–	mā	high level
2nd tone	ˊ	má	middle rising
3rd tone	ˇ	mǎ	falling rising
4th tone	ˋ	mà	high falling

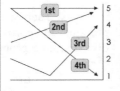

When no tone mark appears above the vowel, then it is a neutral tone.

2. Initials: There are 21 initials in total.

g	Always like g in "go," never like "orange."
s	Always like s in "see," never like "rose."

q	Like in "cheap," but with the lips spread.
x	Like in "sheet," but with the lips spread.
r	Like in "right," but with the lips spread.
z	Like in "kids."
c	Like in "cats."
zh	Like in "jerk."
ch	Like in "church."
sh	Like in "shirt."

*The initials b, p, d, t, k, l, m, n, f, h, j are pronounced approximately like in English, while p, t, k should always be aspirated.

*When you say zh, ch, sh, say it with the tip of your tongue curled back.

3. Finals: There are 35 finals in total. Most of them are pronounced approximately like in English. They can be divided into 5 groups.

	a	Like in "father."
	o	Like in "more."
Simple vowels & diphthongs	e	Like in "her," but stronger. *
	ai	Like in "aisle."
	ei	Like in "eight."
	ao	Like in "how."
	ou	Like in "soul."

Simple vowels plus nasal endings	an	Simple vowel "a" + "n."
	en	Simple vowel "e" + "n."
	ang	Simple vowel "a" + "ng" like in "sing."
	eng	Simple vowel "e" + "ng."
	ong	Like in "long."
Finals beginning with medial "i"	i	Like in "ski." *
	ia, ie, iao, iou*, in, ian, ing, iang, iong	Medial "i" + other finals.
Finals beginning with medial "u"	u	Like in "flute."
	ua, uo, uai, uei*, uan, uen*, uang, ueng	Medial "u" + other finals.
Finals beginning with medial "ü"	ü*	Say "i" as in "ski." Maintain your tongue position, then round your lips and say "u" as in "flute."
	üe, üan, ün	Medial "ü" + other finals.

* The pronunciation of simple vowel "e" differs from the compound vowel "e," like in "ei," "ie," or "uei," in which the "e" should be pronounced like in "let."

* When "i" is preceded by zh, ch, sh, r, z, c, s, it is pronounced like in "sir."
* When "iou," "uei," "uen," is preceded by an initial, it should be changed into "iu," "ui," "un," e.g. "niu," "dui," "sun."
* Only when "ü" is put together with the initials "n, l," the 2 dots should be retained, e.g. "n" + "ü" → "nü," but "x" + "ü" → "xu."
* When finals beginning with a medial are not preceded by any initials, the medial should change its form, e.g. "i" → "yi," "ia" → "ya," "u" → "wu," "ua" → "wa," "ü" → "yu."
* The finals in "sun" & "xun" or "zu" & "ju" look the same, but will be pronounced differently.

Chinese Characters

Chinese writing is represented by "characters," and there are more than 50,000 Chinese characters in existence, of which only about 3,000 are commonly used in daily life.

Chinese words developed into characters formed of strokes from the pictographs cut on oracle bones dating from over 3,000 years ago. The primitive forms of Chinese writing closely resemble the later forms of writing, which became more abstract.

Each character is placed in a square and stands for a meaningful syllable.

Basic Knowledge about Chinese Grammar

1. Parts of Speech

1-1 Nouns

(a) Monosyllabic Words

A monosyllabic word consists of only one character.

【shū】a book, books 【huā】a flower, flowers

(b) Polysyllabic Words

A polysyllabic word consists of more than two characters, which have no separate meaning and should always be bound together as a unit.

【pú】+【táo】=【pútáo】
grapes grapes grapes

(c) Compound Words

A compound word consists of more than two characters, each of which has its own meaning, and it can be divided into two words/morphemes.

【lǐ】 +【wù】 = 【lǐwù】
courtesy thing; substance a present; a gift

(d) The Classifiers

Nouns usually occur with a number and a classifier.

Number Classifier Noun
【wǔ】+【běn】+【shū】=【wǔ běn shū】
 five   books   five books

Classifier	Nouns
liàng	chūzūchē (taxi); gōngjiāochē (bus)
zhī	gǒu (dog); māo (cat)
jiàn	wàitào (coat); máoyī (sweater)

(e) Genitive Particle *de*

wǒ + *de* + shū = wǒ de shū
I   *de*   book   my book, my books

wǒ + mǎi + *de* + shū = wǒ mǎi de shū
I   buy   *de*   book   the book I bought

1-2 Verbs

Chinese verbs have no tense but have various aspects.

(a) *zài* + Verb

Indicates someone is in the process of doing a certain activity.

Tā + 【*zài* + shuìjiào】
s/he   *zài*   sleep
S/he is sleeping.

(b) Verb + *guo*

Indicates that the speaker has had some experience in the past.

Wǒ + 【qù + *guo*】+ Zhōngguó
I   go   *guo*   China
I have been to China before.

(c) Verb + *le*

Indicates that an action has already been completed.

Tā + 【mǎi + *le*】 + yì běn shū
s/he   buy   *le*   a book
S/he bought a book.

(d) Verb + *dào*

Indicates that an action has been begun and has reached a certain stage.

Wǒ + 【zǒu + *dào*】 + xuéxiào
I   walk   *dào*   school
I walked (and reached) the school.

(e) Verb + *de*

Shows the quality of an action that was carried out at a certain point of time in the past.

Wǒ + 【shuì + *de*】 + hěn hǎo
I   sleep   *de*   very good
I slept well.

(f) *yào* + Verb

Indicates the action is going to happen or that the subject wants it to happen in the future.

Wǒ + 【*yào* + kàn】 + jīngjù
I   *yào*   watch   Beijing Opera
I want to watch the Beijing Opera.

(g) *huì* + Verb

(i) Indicates something will occur in the future.

Míngtiān + 【*huì* + xiàyǔ】
tomorrow   *huì*   rain
It will rain tomorrow.

(ii) Shows the ability to do something.

Wǒ + 【huì + shuō】 + Zhōngguóhuà
I   huì   speak   Chinese
I can speak Chinese.

1-3 Adjectives

Put an adjective in front of the noun to make the object more specific in the sentence.

Wǒ + yǒu + 【hěn duō】 + wèntí
I   have   many   questions
I have many questions.

2. Sentence Structure

2-1 Basic Form

The basic structure of a Chinese sentence is SVO.

subject   verb   object
【Wǒ】 + 【xǐhuan】 + 【zhōngguócài】
I   like   Chinese food
I like Chinese food.

2-2 Topic

To describe the topic, add a description after the main subject.

【Wǒ】 + hěn hǎo
I   fine
I'm fine.

【Zhège dìfang】 + hěn duō + rén
this   place   many   people
This place is full of people.

2-3 Time

To indicate a period of time, insert the time word after the subject.

Example: Wǒ kàn shū. (I read a book.)

Wǒ + 【měitiān】 + kàn + shū
I   every day   read   book(s)
I read every day.

2-4 Location

To indicate the location where an action occurred, add the phrase "*zài*" followed by the place word.

Example: Tā qí mótuōchē. (S/he rides motorcycle.)

Tā + 【*zài* + hǎibiān】 + qí + mótuōchē
s/he   *zài*   beach   ride   motorcycle
S/he rides her/his motorcycle at the beach.

2-5 Two Objects after a Verb

The sentence consists of two objects following a single verb. In this pattern, the indirect object is closer to the verb and the direct object follows right after the indirect object.

Wǒ + wèn + 【nǐ】 + 【yí ge wèntí】
I   ask   you   a question
I am asking you a question.

2-6 Serial Actions

The sentence consists of two actions that happened in a
row, in order and without any conjunctions.

Wǒ + 【chūqu】 + 【chīfàn】
I   go out   eat
I went out to eat.

Tā + 【zuò huǒchē】 + 【qù Táiběi】
s/he   take the train   go to Taipei
S/he went to Taipei by train.

2-7 Interrogative Sentences

There are two ways to make an interrogative sentence
in Chinese. You can simply add a question word "*ma*"
and a question mark at the end of the sentence to make
a question, or substitute a question word for the subject
or object in the sentence without altering the sentence
structure.

<Example>
Tā yào mǎi shū.
S/he wants to buy books.

(a) If you want to know if the statement is true, add a
"*ma*" at the end of the sentence.

Tā yào mǎi shū 【*ma*】?
Does s/he want to buy books?

(b) If you want to know who the subject is, substitute "*shéi*" for "tā."

【*Shéi*】yào mǎi shū?
Who wants to buy books?

(c) If you want to know what the object is, substitute "*shénme*" for "shū."

Tā yào mǎi【*shénme*】?
What does s/he want to buy?

(d) If you want to know what event will take place, put "*zuò shénme*" instead of "mǎi shū."

Tā yào【*zuò shénme*】?
What does s/he want to do?

2-8 Situation Changed

If you want to emphasize a change in the situation, add "*le*" at the end of the sentence.

Wǒ méiyǒu qián. → Wǒ méiyǒu qián【*le*】.
I have no money.   I have no money now. (Implying that I had some before, but have spent it all.)

Tā gàosu wǒ. → Tā gàosu wǒ【*le*】.
S/he told me.   S/he has not told me until now.

Xiàyǔ. → Xiàyǔ【*le*】.
It's raining.   It's starting to rain.

Daily Expressions

1 Greetings

Good morning.

Zǎo.
早。

Good afternoon.

Wǔ'ān.
午安。

Good evening.

Wǎn'ān.
晚安。

Hello.

Nín hǎo (Nǐ hǎo).
您好（你好）。

Note 1

"Nín" is the honorific form of "nǐ."

Good morning, Mr. Fisher.

Zǎo, Fisher xiānsheng.
早，Fisher 先生。

How are you?

Nǐ hǎo ma?
你好嗎？

How have you been doing?

Zuìjìn hǎo ma?
最近好嗎？

Are you in good health?

Shēntǐ hǎo ma?
身體好嗎？

How's your family?

Jiārén dōu hǎo ma?
家人都好嗎？

Fine, thank you.

Hěn hǎo, xièxie.
很好，謝謝。

Not bad.

Mǎmahūhū.
馬馬虎虎。

Are you busy these days?

Zuìjìn máng bu máng?
最近忙不忙？

Word Bank ① Address forms

Mr.	▸ xiānsheng	先生
Mrs.	▸ tàitai	太太
Miss	▸ xiǎojie	小姐

Pretty busy.

Tǐng máng de.
挺忙的。

A little bit (busy).

Yǒu yìdiǎr máng.
有一點兒忙。

Not very (busy).

Bú tài máng.
不太忙。

Okay.

Hái xíng.
還行。

Do You Know? ❶ Greet in a Chinese way

When the Chinese greet close friends, they always use greetings such as: "Chīfàn le ma? (Have you eaten?)" or "Shàng nǎr qù? (Where are you off to?)" to show their personal concern.

2 *Appreciation & Apologies*

Thank you.

Xièxie.
謝謝。

I really appreciate it.

Zhēnshì tài gǎnxiè le!
真是太感謝了！

Thanks for your invitation.

Xièxie nǐ de yāoqǐng.
謝謝你的邀請。

Your assistance is highly appreciated.

Xièxie nǐ de bāngmáng.
謝謝你的幫忙。

That's very nice of you.

Nǐ zhēn hǎo.
你真好。

I have given you so much trouble.

Máfan nǐ le.
麻煩你了。

I can't thank you enough.

Gǎnjī bú jìn.
感激不盡。

You are welcome.

Bú kèqi.

不客氣。

That's nothing.

Méi shénme!

沒什麼！

It's my pleasure.

Zhè shì wǒ de róngxìng.

這是我的榮幸。

I am happy to be of some help.

Hěn gāoxìng wǒ bāng de shàng máng.

很高興我幫得上忙。

You speak very good Chinese.

Nǐ de Zhōngwén shuō de zhēn hǎo.

你的中文說得真好。

Not at all.

Nǎli, nǎli.

哪裡，哪裡。

Excuse me.

Bù hǎo yìsi.

不好意思。

I am sorry.

Duìbuqǐ.

對不起。

Sorry for being late.

Duìbuqǐ, wǒ lái wǎn le.

對不起，我來晚了。

It's all my fault.

Dōu shì wǒ bù hǎo.

都是我不好。

Don't be upset.

Bié shēngqì.

別生氣。

I didn't mean it.

Wǒ bú shì gùyì de.

我不是故意的。

Forgive me, please.

Qǐng yuánliàng wǒ.

請原諒我。

Please accept my sincere apologies.

Wǒ chéngxīn-chéngyì de xiàng nín dàoqiàn.

我誠心誠意地向您道歉。

That's all right.

Méi guānxi.

沒關係。

Never mind.

Bié zàiyì.

別在意。

3 *Saying Goodbye*

I am going.

Wǒ zǒu le.

我走了。

Sorry, I've got to go now.

Bù hǎo yìsi, wǒ děi xiān zǒu le.

不好意思，我得先走了。

Goodbye.

Zàijiàn.

再見。

Note 2

Although "zàijiàn," the traditional way of saying goodbye is still commonly used, the imported "bye-bye" is also heard everywhere.

See you tomorrow.

Míngtiān jiàn.

明天見。

See you next time.

Gǎitiān jiàn.

改天見。

See you later.

Yíhuìr jiàn.
一會兒見。

Good night.

Wǎn'ān.
晚安。

Good luck to you.

Zhù nǐ hǎo yùn.
祝你好運。

Take care.

Duō bǎozhòng.
多保重。

Be careful.

Lùshang xiǎoxīn.
路上小心。

Thank you, and you too.

Xièxie, nǐ yě yíyàng.
謝謝，你也一樣。

Please say hello to Cindy for me.

Qǐng dài wǒ xiàng Cindy wènhǎo.
請代我向 Cindy 問好。

Bon voyage.

Yílù-shùnfēng.
一路順風。

4 *Inquiries & Requests*

What time is it, please?

Qǐngwèn xiànzài jǐ diǎn?
請問現在幾點？

May I speak to Mr. Wang, please?

Qǐngwèn Wáng xiānsheng zài ma?
請問王先生在嗎？

Note 3

"Qǐngwèn" means literally, "May I ask you, please?" Add this phrase before your questions to make your inquiry sound more polite.

How do I get to this restaurant?

Zhèi jiā cāntīng zěnme zǒu?
這家餐廳怎麼走？

How do I get to the railroad station?

Huǒchēzhàn zěnme zǒu?
火車站怎麼走？

Where is the department store?

Bǎihuò gōngsī zài nǎli?
百貨公司在哪裡？

Where can I get the ticket?

Zài nǎli mǎi piào?

在哪裡買票？

Is there a convenience store near here?

Zhèr yǒu méiyǒu biànlì shāngdiàn?

這兒有沒有便利商店？

Is there a restroom around?

Zhèr yǒu méiyǒu wèishēngjiān?

這兒有沒有衛生間？

Would you please do me a favor?

Kěyǐ bāng wǒ yí ge máng ma?

可以幫我一個忙嗎？

Do you accept a credit card?

Kěyǐ shuākǎ ma?

可以刷卡嗎？

Where can I buy these things?

Qù nǎli kěyǐ mǎi dào zhèixiē dōngxi?

去哪裡可以買到這些東西？

Where can I get this Chinese dish?

Qù nǎli kěyǐ chī dào zhèi dào zhōngguócài?

去哪裡可以吃到這道中國菜？

Are you American?

Nǐ shì bu shì měiguórén?

你是不是美國人？

Can you speak English?

Nǐ huì bu huì shuō Yīngwén?

你會不會說英文？

When is the bus coming?

Gōngjiāochē shénme shíhou lái?

公交車什麼時候來？

When will you get there?

Nǐ shénme shíhou qù?

你什麼時候去？

How much is this?

Zhèige duōshao qián?

這個多少錢？

How much are those together?

Yígòng duōshao qián?

一共多少錢？

How long will it take to walk over there?

Zǒu guoqu yào duōjiǔ shíjiān?

走過去要多久時間？

How long will it take to get to the hotel from the airport by taxi?

Cóng jīchǎng dào fàndiàn zuò chūzūchē yào duōjiǔ shíjiān?

從機場到飯店坐出租車要多久時間？

Speak a little more slowly, please.

Qǐng màn yìdiǎr shuō.
請慢一點兒說。

Say it again, please.

Qǐng zài shuō yícì.
請再說一次。

Wait a moment, please.

Qǐng děng yíxià.
請等一下。

Hold my luggage, please.

Qǐng bāng wǒ ná xíngli.
請幫我拿行李。

Give me another glass, please.

Qǐng bāng wǒ huàn bēizi.
請幫我換杯子。

Give me a glass of water, please.

Qǐng gěi wǒ yì bēi shuǐ.
請給我一杯水。

Give me a cup of coffee and a packet of sugar, please.

Qǐng gěi wǒ yì bēi kāfēi hé yì bāo táng.
請給我一杯咖啡和一包糖。

I'd like to eat Chinese food.

Wǒ xiǎng chī zhōngguócài.

我想吃中國菜。

I'd like to see a Chinese movie.

Wǒ xiǎng kàn zhōngguó diànyǐng.

我想看中國電影。

I want this one.

Wǒ yào zhèige.

我要這個。

I want a hamburger.

Wǒ yào yí ge hànbǎo.

我要一個漢堡。

I want to buy two tickets for the movie.

Wǒ yào mǎi liǎng zhāng diànyǐngpiào.

我要買兩張電影票。

I want to go to Beijing. Please give me a ticket for the train.

Wǒ yào qù Běijīng, qǐng gěi wǒ yì zhāng huǒchēpiào.

我要去北京，請給我一張火車票。

Note 4

"Wǒ yào," or "I want...." is a very useful phrase. Whatever you want or want to do, just precede it with "wǒ yào" and you will be understood.

14

Numbers, Dates & Time

一	一 1	八	六 6
二	二 2	十	七 7
三	三 3	八	八 8
三	四 4	𠂆	九 9
X	五 5	|	十 10

1 *Counting*

Word Bank 2 Basic figures

0	▶ líng	零、○
1	▶ yī	一
2	▶ èr, liǎng	二、兩
3	▶ sān	三
4	▶ sì	四
5	▶ wǔ	五
6	▶ liù	六
7	▶ qī	七
8	▶ bā	八
9	▶ jiǔ	九
10	▶ shí	十
11	▶ shíyī	十一
12	▶ shí'èr	十二
13	▶ shísān	十三
14	▶ shísì	十四
15	▶ shíwǔ	十五
16	▶ shíliù	十六
17	▶ shíqī	十七

18	▶ shíbā	十八
19	▶ shíjiǔ	十九
20	▶ èrshí	二十
21	▶ èrshíyī	二十一
30	▶ sānshí	三十
40	▶ sìshí	四十
50	▶ wǔshí	五十
60	▶ liùshí	六十
70	▶ qīshí	七十
80	▶ bāshí	八十
90	▶ jiǔshí	九十
100	▶ yìbǎi	一百

NUMBERS, DATES & TIME

Note 5

When followed by a measure word, "2" is pronounced as "liǎng," such as "liǎng ge rén (two persons)" or "liǎng zhāng piào (two tickets)." However, the figure two is read "èr (2)" if no measure word goes immediately after it such as "èrshí (20)," "èrbǎi (200)," "èrqiān (2,000)." In Taiwan, people say "liǎngbǎi (200)," "liǎngqiān (2,000)," instead, but "liǎngshí (20)" is never allowed.

Word Bank 3 Calculation

15	▶ 10+5	▶ shíwǔ	十五
37	▶ 30+7	▶ sānshíqī	三十七
58	▶ 50+8	▶ wǔshíbā	五十八
71	▶ 70+1	▶ qīshíyī	七十一
94	▶ 90+4	▶ jiǔshísì	九十四
132	▶ 100+30+2	▶ yìbǎi sānshí'èr	一百三十二
220	▶ 200+20	▶ liǎngbǎi èrshí	兩百二十
348	▶ 300+40+8	▶ sānbǎi sìshíbā	三百四十八
480	▶ 400+80	▶ sìbǎi bāshí	四百八十
560	▶ 500+60	▶ wǔbǎi liùshí	五百六十
610	▶ 600+10	▶ liùbǎi yīshí	六百一十
730	▶ 700+30	▶ qībǎi sānshí	七百三十
802	▶ 800+0+2	▶ bābǎi líng èr	八百零二
950	▶ 900+50	▶ jiǔbǎi wǔshí	九百五十

Note 6

Chinese numbers are easy. As you can see above, 15 is "10+5," 94 is "90+4," and 950 is "900+50." Learn the principles and you should be able to say any number you want.

Word Bank ④ Large sums

1,000	▶ yìqiān	一千
10,000	▶ yíwàn	一萬
100,000	▶ shíwàn	十萬
1,000,000	▶ yìbǎi wàn	一百萬
10,000,000	▶ yìqiān wàn	一千萬
100,000,000	▶ yíyì	一億

NUMBERS, DATES & TIME

Word Bank ⑤ Calculation of large sums

30,000	▶ 3 × 10,000	▶ sānwàn	三萬
600,000	▶ 60 × 10,000	▶ liùshí wàn	六十萬
850,000	▶ 85 × 10,000	▶ bāshíwǔ wàn	八十五萬
2,000,000	▶ 200 × 10,000	▶ liǎngbǎi wàn	兩百萬
5,000,000	▶ 500 × 10,000	▶ wǔbǎi wàn	五百萬
8,000,000	▶ 800 × 10,000	▶ bābǎi wàn	八百萬
40,000,000	▶ 4,000 × 10,000	▶ sìqiān wàn	四千萬
73,000,000	▶ 7,300 × 10,000	▶ qīqiān sānbǎi wàn	七千三百萬
500,000,000	▶ 5 × 100,000,000	▶ wǔ yì	五億
4,000,000,000	▶ 40 × 100,000,000	▶ sìshí yì	四十億

Do You Know? ❷ 10,000 ≠ ten thousand

Instead of "thousand" in English, "**wàn** (10,000 / ten thousand)" is the basic unit of calculation for large sums in Chinese. Therefore, "a hundred thousand" should be "**shíwàn**" (10 × **wàn**), while a million is "**bǎiwàn**" (100 × **wàn**) and ten million is "**qiānwàn**" (1,000 × **wàn**). Another even larger unit called "**yì**" is required when calculating sums larger than a hundred million.

Word Bank ❻ Ordinals

first	▶ dì+1	▶ dì-yī	第一
second	▶ dì+2	▶ dì-èr	第二
third	▶ dì+3	▶ dì-sān	第三
fourth	▶ dì+4	▶ dì-sì	第四
fifth	▶ dì+5	▶ dì-wǔ	第五
sixth	▶ dì+6	▶ dì-liù	第六
twelfth	▶ dì+12	▶ dì-shí'èr	第十二
thirty second	▶ dì+32	▶ dì-sānshí'èr	第三十二
one hundredth	▶ dì+100	▶ dì-yìbǎi	第一百

Note 7

To form ordinals, all you have to do is to put the prefix "dì" in front of the cardinals.

Word Bank 7 About quantity

nothing	▶ shénme dōu méiyǒu	什麼都沒有
few	▶ hěn shǎo	很少
a little	▶ yìdiǎr	一點兒
some	▶ yìxiē	一些
many	▶ hěn duō	很多
enough	▶ gòu le	夠了
not enough	▶ bú gòu	不夠
too much	▶ tài duō le	太多了
too little	▶ tài shǎo le	太少了
more	▶ duō yìdiǎr	多一點兒
less	▶ shǎo yìdiǎr	少一點兒

Do You Know? ❸ "4" is a big trouble

Do you know how 44 stone lions and the Chinese people are related? There is a very interesting tongue twister, which is meant to train people to distinguish the number 40 (sìshí) and 14 (shísì). Difficult enough itself, the author adds "shíshīzi (stone lions)" into the rhyme, which makes correct pronunciation an even bigger challenge. Don't think that this is just for fun. If you mistake "No.4 (sì hào)" for "No.10 (shí hào)" when you are asking for directions, you most probably will get lost. Or when at a cashier, if you mistake "14 dollars (shísì kuài qián)" for "40 dollars (sìshí kuài qián)," then you definitely will suffer from a great loss.

By the way, you might find that in some buildings, especially in hospitals or hotels, there is no such thing as a fourth floor. This is because, the number "4," pronounced as "sì," sounds almost the same as "death (sǐ)," and no one would like to stay in a place that seems to say you are "doomed to die."

23

NUMBERS, DATES & TIME

2 Dates

Word Bank 8 About date

one day	▶ yì tiān	一天
today	▶ jīntiān	今天
tomorrow	▶ míngtiān	明天
yesterday	▶ zuótiān	昨天
the day after tomorrow	▶ hòutiān	後天
the day before yesterday	▶ qiántiān	前天
three days later	▶ sān tiān hòu	三天後
five days ago	▶ wǔ tiān qián	五天前

Word Bank 9 About year

one year	▶ yì nián	一年
this year	▶ jīnnián	今年
next year	▶ míngnián	明年
last year	▶ qùnián	去年
the year after next	▶ hòunián	後年

the year before last	▶ qiánnián	前年
three years later	▶ sān nián hòu	三年後
five years ago	▶ wǔ nián qián	五年前

Word Bank 10 About month

one month	▶ yí ge yuè	一個月
two months	▶ liǎng ge yuè	兩個月
three months	▶ sān ge yuè	三個月
this month	▶ zhèige yuè	這個月
last month	▶ shàng ge yuè	上個月
next month	▶ xià ge yuè	下個月
three months later	▶ sān ge yuè hòu	三個月後
five months ago	▶ wǔ ge yuè qián	五個月前

Word Bank 11 About week

one week	▶ yí ge xīngqī	一個星期
two weeks	▶ liǎng ge xīngqī	兩個星期
three weeks	▶ sān ge xīngqī	三個星期
this week	▶ zhèige xīngqī	這個星期
last week	▶ shàng ge xīngqī	上個星期
next week	▶ xià ge xīngqī	下個星期
three weeks later	▶ sān ge xīngqī hòu	三個星期後
five weeks ago	▶ wǔ ge xīngqī qián	五個星期前

 **Word Bank 12 Days of the week**

Monday	▶ xīngqīyī	星期一
Tuesday	▶ xīngqī'èr	星期二
Wednesday	▶ xīngqīsān	星期三
Thursday	▶ xīngqīsì	星期四
Friday	▶ xīngqīwǔ	星期五
Saturday	▶ xīngqīliù	星期六
Sunday	▶ xīngqītiān	星期天

Note 8

"Xīngqī," can be substituted by "lǐbài" in colloquial Chinese.

Word Bank 13 Months of the year

January	▶ yīyuè	一月
February	▶ èryuè	二月
March	▶ sānyuè	三月
April	▶ sìyuè	四月
May	▶ wǔyuè	五月
June	▶ liùyuè	六月
July	▶ qīyuè	七月
August	▶ bāyuè	八月
September	▶ jiǔyuè	九月
October	▶ shíyuè	十月
November	▶ shíyīyuè	十一月
December	▶ shí'èryuè	十二月

NUMBERS, DATES & TIME

Do You Know? ❹ **How to give a date**

✻ This is how to give dates:
year (nián) → month (yuè) → date
(hào) → day of the week (xīngqī)

✻ Example:

NOV						2010
Sun	Mon	Tue	Wed	Thu	Fri	Sat
	1	2	3	4	5	6
7	8	9	10	11	12	13
14	15	16	17	18	19	20
21	22	23	24	25	26	27
28	29	30				

Today is Thursday, November 18, 2010.
Jīntiān shì èr líng yī líng nián shíyīyuè shíbā
hào xīngqīsì.

今天是 2010 年 11 月 18 號星期四。

✻ In Chinese, the first day of a week is Monday instead of Sunday. Therefore, "xià ge xīngqītiān," literally means "next Sunday," and would be "two weeks from now" instead of "this upcoming Sunday." (It refers to November 28, not 21.)

What is today's date?

Jīntiān shì jǐ hào?
今天是幾號？

Today is June 2.

Jīntiān shì liùyuè èr hào.
今天是六月二號。

Is today Friday?

Jīntiān shì xīngqīwǔ ma?
今天是星期五嗎？

No, yesterday was Friday. Today is Saturday.

Búshì, zuótiān shì xīngqīwǔ. Jīntiān shì xīngqīliù.
不是，昨天是星期五。今天是星期六。

I was in Beijing last month.

Wǒ shàng ge yuè zài Běijīng.
我上個月在北京。

I will be in Shanghai next week.

Wǒ xià ge xīngqī yào qù Shànghǎi.
我下個星期要去上海。

When did you arrive?

Nǐ shì shénme shíhou dào de?
你是什麼時候到的？

I arrived 2 days ago.

Wǒ shì liǎng tiān qián dào de.
我是兩天前到的。

I'd like to stay for one week.

Wǒ dǎsuàn zhù yí ge xīngqī.
我打算住一個星期。

When are you leaving?

Nǐ shénme shíhou líkāi?
你什麼時候離開？

I will be leaving 3 days later.

Wǒ sān tiān hòu líkāi.
我三天後離開。

I will be leaving one day early.

Wǒ yào zǎo yì tiān líkāi.
我要早一天離開。

What season is it now?

Xiànzài shì shénme jìjié?
現在是什麼季節？

It's spring.

Xiànzài shì chūntiān.
現在是春天。

In which year were you born?

Nǐ shì nǎ yì nián chūshēng de?
你是哪一年出生的？

I was born in 1985.

Wǒ shì yī jiǔ bā wǔ nián chūshēng de.

我是 1985 年出生的。

When do you have free time?

Nǐ něi tiān yǒu kòng?

你哪天有空？

I am free tomorrow.

Wǒ míngtiān yǒu kòng.

我明天有空。

Sorry, I am very busy these days.

Duìbuqǐ, wǒ zuìjìn méi kòng.

對不起，我最近沒空。

How long are you going to stay?

Nǐ dǎsuàn dāi duōjiǔ?

你打算待多久？

I will stay for 5 days.

Wǒ dǎsuàn dāi wǔ tiān.

我打算待五天。

Word Bank 14 Seasons

spring	▶ chūntiān	春天
summer	▶ xiàtiān	夏天
autumn	▶ qiūtiān	秋天
winter	▶ dōngtiān	冬天

Do You Know? 5 Propitious and auspicious dates

The Chinese people believe that time has an influential power on one's well-being. Therefore, it's important for the Chinese people to choose a lucky day, i.e. "huángdào jírì" for all kinds of important events, such as a wedding, moving houses, inauguration of a shop, etc. Most Chinese families keep a very special almanac, or "huánglì," at home. It tells you all the propitious days during that particular year. So if you come upon many weddings or you find all the restaurants are fully booked, then you know it must be a "good day."

3 *Time*

Word Bank 15 Basic terms about time

morning	▶ zǎoshang	早上
noon	▶ zhōngwǔ	中午
afternoon	▶ xiàwǔ	下午
evening	▶ wǎnshang	晚上
midnight	▶ bànyè	半夜
before dawn	▶ língchén	凌晨
daytime	▶ báitiān	白天
nighttime	▶ yèlǐ	夜裡
now	▶ xiànzài	現在
just now	▶ gāngcái	剛才
later	▶ dāihuìr	待會兒
recently	▶ zuìjìn	最近
already	▶ yǐjīng	已經
not yet	▶ hái méi	還沒
hour	▶ xiǎoshí / zhōngtóu	小時/鐘頭
minute	▶ fēnzhōng	分鐘
second	▶ miǎo	秒

NUMBERS, DATES & TIME

Do You Know? **6** How to tell the time

※ This is how to tell the time:
hour (diǎn) → minute (fēn)

※ Example:

07 : 20 (a.m.)	7+diǎn+ 20+fēn	zǎoshang qī diǎn èrshí fēn	早上 7 點 20 分
08 : 00 (a.m.)	8+diǎn	zǎoshang bā diǎn	早上 8 點
09 : 30 (a.m.)	9+diǎn +bàn	zǎoshang jiǔ diǎn bàn	早上 9 點半
12 : 05 (p.m.)	12+diǎn+ 5+fēn	zhōngwǔ shí'èr diǎn wǔ fēn	中午 12 點 5 分
04 : 10 (p.m.)	4+diǎn+ 10+fēn	xiàwǔ sì diǎn shí fēn	下午 4 點 10 分
10 : 50 (p.m.)	10+diǎn+ 50+fēn	wǎnshang shí diǎn wǔshí fēn	晚上 10 點 50 分

What time is it?

Xiànzài jǐ diǎn?

現在幾點？

It's 7:15.

Xiànzài qī diǎn shíwǔ fēn.

現在七點十五分。

It's nearly nine.

Xiànzài kuài jiǔ diǎn le.

現在快九點了。

When does it start?

Shénme shíhou kāishǐ?

什麼時候開始？

It starts at 5:30.

Wǔ diǎn bàn kāishǐ.

五點半開始。

It's already over.

Yǐjīng jiéshù le.

已經結束了。

My watch is 5 minutes slow.

Wǒ de biǎo màn wǔ fēnzhōng.

我的錶慢五分鐘。

Can you make it by 4:00 p.m.?

Xiàwǔ sì diǎn néng bu néng dào?

下午四點能不能到？

No, we can't. It won't arrive until tomorrow morning.

Bù néng, míngtiān zǎoshang cái néng dào.

不能，明天早上才能到。

Let's meet at the Fuxingmen Subway Station.

Wǒmen yuē zài Fùxīngmén Zhàn jiànmiàn ba!

我們約在復興門站見面吧！

When?

Shénme shíhou?

什麼時候？

Tonight at 7:00 p.m.

Jīntiān wǎnshang qī diǎn.

今天晚上七點。

Can you make it earlier?

Kěyǐ zǎo yìdiǎn ma?

可以早一點嗎？

Can you make it later?

Kěyǐ wǎn yìdiǎn ma?

可以晚一點嗎？

When is the next train/bus, please?

Qǐngwèn, xià yì bān chē shénme shíhou kāi?

請問，下一班車什麼時候開？

The next train/bus leaves at 7:30.

Xià yì bān chē qī diǎn bàn kāi.

下一班車七點半開。

When does the store open?

Zhèr jǐ diǎn kāimén?

這兒幾點開門？

It opens at 8:00.

Zhèr bā diǎn kāimén.

這兒八點開門。

The store is open 24 hours.

Zhèr èrshísì xiǎoshí yíngyè.

這兒二十四小時營業。

It's been one hour.

Yǐjīng guòle yí ge zhōngtóu.

已經過了一個鐘頭。

One moment, please.

Qǐng nǐ děng yíxià.

請你等一下。

I'll be back in 5 minutes.

Wǒ wǔ fēnzhōng hòu huílai.

我五分鐘後回來。

How long does it take?

Xūyào duōjiǔ?

需要多久？

It takes 10 minutes.

Xūyào shí fēnzhōng.

需要十分鐘。

It will be ready right away.

Mǎshàng jiù hǎo le.

馬上就好了。

Do You Know? 7 The Chinese zodiac

Ask a Chinese, "What's your zodiac animal sign?" He will tell you that "Mine is a horse" or "Mine is a dog." Some would even insist that he has inherited certain characteristics of that particular animal. This is because the Chinese people believe that 12 animals in the heavens take turns controlling the ups and downs of one particular year. This cycle of twelve is called "The Twelve Animal Signs." For instance, 1972 was the Year of the Rat, while 1973 was the Year of the Ox, followed in order by the Year of the Tiger, Rabbit, Dragon, Snake, Horse, Goat, Monkey, Rooster, Dog, and Boar. Moreover, as Chinese people have a preference for dragons, many people try hard to have a baby born in the Year of the Dragon, so there is this "Baby Boom" in Dragon years.

Reservations

1 *Booking a Hotel*

I'd like to reserve a room.

Wǒ yào dìng yí ge fángjiān.
我要訂一個房間。

When would you like the reservation for?

Nín yào dìng shénme shíhou de?
您要訂什麼時候的？

How many days do you want to stay?

Nín yào zhù jǐ tiān?
您要住幾天？

I want to stay for 3 days.

Wǒ yào zhù sān tiān.
我要住三天。

From March 15 until March 17.

Cóng sānyuè shíwǔ hào dào sānyuè shíqī hào.
從三月十五號到三月十七號。 see p.27

What kind of room would you like?

Nín yào dìng jǐ rén fáng?
您要訂幾人房？

I'd like to book a single room.

Wǒ yào dìng dānrénfáng.
我要訂單人房。

Word Bank 16 Room types

dormitory	▶ duōrénfáng	多人房
double bed	▶ shuāngrénchuáng	雙人床
economy room	▶ pǔtōngfáng	普通房
single	▶ dānrénfáng	單人房
standard room	▶ biāozhǔnfáng	標準房
suite	▶ tàofáng	套房
twin	▶ shuāngrénfáng	雙人房

Please give me your full name.

Qǐngwèn nín de dàmíng shì......?

請問您的大名是……？

My name is Peter Fisher.

Wǒ jiào Peter Fisher.

我叫 Peter Fisher。

May I ask you to first pay a deposit of 500 dollars?

Máfan nín yùfù dìngjīn wǔbǎi kuài.

麻煩您預付訂金五百塊。

May I pay with a credit card?

Kěyǐ shuākǎ ma?

可以刷卡嗎？

Yes. Here is your receipt.

Kěyǐ. Zhè shì nín de shōujù.

可以。這是您的收據。

I have already booked a room.

Wǒ yǐjīng yùdìngle yí ge fángjiān.

我已經預訂了一個房間。

I want to cancel my reservation.

Wǒ yào qǔxiāo yùdìng de fángjiān.

我要取消預訂的房間。

I'd like to move to a different room.

Wǒ yào huàn yí ge fángjiān.

我要換一個房間。

I want a cheaper room.

Wǒ yào piányi yìdiǎr de fángjiān.

我要便宜一點兒的房間。

I'd like a bigger room.

Wǒ yào dà yìdiǎr de fángjiān.

我要大一點兒的房間。

I want to change the date of my reservation.

Wǒ yào gēnggǎi dìngfáng de rìqī.

我要更改訂房的日期。

Make it March 20.

Gǎichéng sānyuè èrshí hào.

改成三月二十號。

Sorry, there are no vacant rooms.

Duìbuqǐ, méiyǒu kōng fángjiān le.

對不起，沒有空房間了。

We are fully booked.

Yǐjīng kèmǎn le.

已經客滿了。

Sorry, I don't have a record of your reservation.

Duìbuqǐ, méiyǒu nín de dìngfáng jìlù.

對不起，沒有您的訂房紀錄。

Do I have free access to the Internet?

Kěyǐ miǎnfèi shàngwǎng ma?

可以免費上網嗎？

For more expressions about accommodations, please see pp.89-110.

Word Bank ⑰ Hotel types

B & B	▶ mínsù	民宿
five-star hotel	▶ wǔxīngjí fàndiàn	五星級飯店
guesthouse	▶ zhāodàisuǒ	招待所
motel	▶ qìchē lǚguǎn	汽車旅館
three-star hotel	▶ sānxīngjí fàndiàn	三星級飯店
youth hostel	▶ qīngnián lǚguǎn	青年旅館

2 *Booking a Restaurant*

I want to book a table for tomorrow night.

Wǒ yào dìng míngtiān wǎnshang de wèizi.

我要訂明天晚上的位子。

For how many people, please?

Qǐngwèn jǐ wèi?

請問幾位？

Eight people.

Bā ge rén.

八個人。

What is your surname?

Guìxìng?

貴姓？

My surname is Fisher.

Wǒ xìng Fisher.

我姓 Fisher。

Mr. Fisher, what time would you like the reservation for?

Fisher xiānsheng, nín shénme shíhou dào?

Fisher 先生，您什麼時候到？

About 7:00 p.m.

Chàbuduō wǎnshang qī diǎn dào.
差不多晚上七點到。

OK, I will hold the table until 7:00 p.m.

Hǎode, wǒ tì nín bǎoliú dào qī diǎn.
好的，我替您保留到七點。

I'd like a table by the window.

Wǒ yào kào chuāng de wèizi.
我要靠窗的位子。

I'd like a table by the wall.

Wǒ yào kào qiáng de wèizi.
我要靠牆的位子。

I'd like to book a room.

Wǒ yào dìng yì jiān bāoxiāng.
我要訂一間包廂。

Sorry, we are fully booked.

Duìbuqǐ, yǐjīng kèmǎn le.
對不起，已經客滿了。

What is the minimum charge?

Zuìdī xiāofèi duōshao qián?
最低消費多少錢？

For more expressions about eating, please see pp.111-128.

RESERVATIONS

3 Booking a Show

Are there any Beijing Opera performances on May 8?

Wǔyuè bā hào yǒu jīngjù biǎoyǎn ma?

五月八號有京劇表演嗎？

I'd like to buy tickets for the show on May 8.

Wǒ yào mǎi wǔyuè bā hào de piào.

我要買五月八號的票。

What price of ticket do you want to buy?

Nín yào mǎi něi yì zhǒng piàojià de?

您要買哪一種票價的？

I'll take two 100-dollar tickets.

Yìbǎi kuài de liǎng zhāng.

一百塊的兩張。

Please give me seats towards the middle.

Qǐng gěi wǒ zhōngjiān de wèizi.

請給我中間的位子。

Please give me seats in the first row.

Qǐng gěi wǒ dì-yī pái de wèizi.

請給我第一排的位子。

This performance has 3 showings in all.

Zhèige biǎoyǎn yígòng yǒu sān chǎng.

這個表演一共有三場。

Where is the box office?

Shòupiàochù zài nǎr?

售票處在哪兒？

I want to book tickets over the phone.

Wǒ yào diànhuà dìngpiào.

我要電話訂票。

Please deliver the tickets to my hotel.

Qǐng bǎ piào sòng dào wǒ de lǚguǎn.

請把票送到我的旅館。

This is the address of the hotel.

Zhè shì lǚguǎn de dìzhǐ.

這是旅館的地址。

You can use your passport to collect the tickets.

Nín kěyǐ píng hùzhào lái lǐng piào.

您可以憑護照來領票。

Please arrive at the performance one hour earlier.

Qǐng tízǎo yí ge xiǎoshí rùchǎng.

請提早一個小時入場。

★ For more expressions about going to a show, please see pp.134-139.

4 *Renting a Car*

I want to rent a car.

Wǒ yào zū yí liàng chē.

我要租一輛車。

When do you need it for?

Nín shénme shíhou yào yòng?

您什麼時候要用？

From September 6 to September 10.

Jiǔyuè liù hào dào jiǔyuè shí hào.

九月六號到九月十號。

Here is our catalog. Which type of car would you like?

Zhèr yǒu mùlù, nín yào nǎ yì zhǒng chē?

這兒有目錄，您要哪一種車？

How much is this model?

Zhèi zhǒng chē duōshao qián?

這種車多少錢？

500 dollars per day.

Yì tiān wǔbǎi kuài.

一天五百塊。

Does that include insurance?

Hán bǎoxiǎn ma?

含保險嗎？

Can you make it a bit cheaper?

Kěyǐ zài piányi yìdiǎr ma?

可以再便宜一點兒嗎？

Is it possible to have a test drive?

Kěyǐ shì chē ma?

可以試車嗎？

Are there any 9-seater cars?

Yǒu méiyǒu jiǔrénzuò de chē?

有沒有九人座的車？

I would like to have a car with better performance.

Wǒ yào xìngnéng hǎo yìdiǎr de chē.

我要性能好一點兒的車。

Please give me your passport and driver's license.

Qǐng gěi wǒ nín de hùzhào hé jiàzhào.

請給我您的護照和駕照。

Do you have an international driver's license?

Nín yǒu méiyǒu guójì jiàzhào?

您有沒有國際駕照？

Please fill out this form.

Qǐng tián yíxià zhè fèn biǎogé.

請填一下這份表格。

Please give me some ID as security.

Qǐng yā zhèngjiàn.
請押證件。

How much is the deposit?

Yājīn duōshao qián?
押金多少錢？

You can return the car in Beijing.

Nín kěyǐ zài Běijīng huán chē.
您可以在北京還車。

Do you have an emergency contact number?

Yǒu méiyǒu jǐnjí liánluò diànhuà?
有沒有緊急聯絡電話？

Do you have a towing service?

Yǒu méiyǒu tuōdiào fúwù?
有沒有拖吊服務？

What happens if the car breaks down?

Chēzi gùzhàng zěnmebàn?
車子故障怎麼辦？

What kind of gas does this car use?

Yào jiā shénme qìyóu?
要加什麼汽油？

> For more expressions about driving a car, please see pp.71-73.

Transportation

1 *Asking for Directions*

How do I get to Heping Hotel, please?

Qǐngwèn, dào Hépíng Fàndiàn zěnme zǒu?

請問，到和平飯店怎麼走？

You will have to turn left over there.

Qiánmian zuǒ zhuǎn.

前面左轉。

When you pass the traffic lights, turn right.

Guòle hónglùdēng yǐhòu yòu zhuǎn.

過了紅綠燈以後右轉。

Please draw me a map.

Qǐng huà dìtú gěi wǒ kàn.

請畫地圖給我看。

Where does this street lead to?

Zhè tiáo lù dào shénme dìfang?

這條路到什麼地方？

I've lost my way.

Wǒ mílù le.

我迷路了。

Where is this place?

Zhèr shì nǎr?

這兒是哪兒？

Word Bank 18 Direction

go straight	▶ yìzhí zǒu	一直走
go back the way you came	▶ wǎng huí zǒu	往回走
keep to the left	▶ kào zuǒbian	靠左邊
keep to the right	▶ kào yòubian	靠右邊
turn left	▶ zuǒ zhuǎn	左轉
turn right	▶ yòu zhuǎn	右轉

Word Bank 19 On the road

bridge	▶ qiáo	橋
circle	▶ zhuànpán	轉盤
	▶ yuánhuán	圓環
forked road	▶ chàlù	岔路
lane	▶ xiàngzi	巷子
one-way street	▶ dānxíngdào	單行道
overpass	▶ tiānqiáo	天橋
road sign	▶ lùbiāo	路標
sidewalk	▶ rénxíngdào	人行道
traffic lights	▶ hónglǜdēng	紅綠燈
tunnel	▶ suìdào	隧道
underpass	▶ dìxiàdào	地下道

TRANSPORTATION

53

This is Zhongshan North Road.

Zhèr shì Zhōngshān Běilù.

這兒是中山北路。

Are there any hotels nearby?

Fùjìn yǒu méiyǒu lǚguǎn?

附近有沒有旅館？

It's right up ahead.

Jiù zài qiánmian.

就在前面。

(Pulling out a map) Please point it out for me.

Qǐng nǐ zhǐ gěi wǒ kàn.

請你指給我看。

Can you lead the way?

Nǐ kěyǐ dàilù ma?

你可以帶路嗎？

Is it far from here?

Lí zhèr yuǎn bu yuǎn?

離這兒遠不遠？

It's very close.

Hěn jìn.

很近。

Word Bank ⑳ Places you may go

bank	▶ yínháng	銀行
bus stop	▶ gōngjiāozhàn	公交站
	▶ gōngchēzhàn	公車站
department store	▶ bǎihuò gōngsī	百貨公司
embassy	▶ dàshǐguǎn	大使館
hospital	▶ yīyuàn	醫院
hotel	▶ lǚguǎn	旅館
library	▶ túshūguǎn	圖書館
MRT station	▶ jiéyùnzhàn	捷運站
museum	▶ bówùguǎn	博物館
night market	▶ yèshì	夜市
park	▶ gōngyuán	公園
police station	▶ jǐngchájú	警察局
post office	▶ yóujú	郵局
railroad station	▶ huǒchēzhàn	火車站
restaurant	▶ cāntīng	餐廳
restroom	▶ wèishēngjiān	衛生間
	▶ xǐshǒujiān	洗手間
square	▶ guǎngchǎng	廣場
subway station	▶ dìtiězhàn	地鐵站
teahouse	▶ cháguǎnr	茶館兒

TRANSPORTATION

| temple | ▶ sìmiào | 寺廟 |
| ticket office | ▶ shòupiàochù | 售票處 |

Word Bank 21 Indicating locations

up ahead	▶ qiánmian	前面
back there	▶ hòumian	後面
left	▶ zuǒbian	左邊
right	▶ yòubian	右邊
side	▶ pángbiān	旁邊
opposite side	▶ duìmiàn	對面
east	▶ dōngbian	東邊
west	▶ xībian	西邊
south	▶ nánbian	南邊
north	▶ běibian	北邊
above	▶ shàngmian	上面
below	▶ xiàmian	下面
bottom	▶ dǐxia	底下
inside	▶ lǐmian	裡面
outside	▶ wàimian	外面
here	▶ zhèli	這裡

there	▸ nàli	那裡
that direction	▸ nàge fāngxiàng	那個方向
nearby	▸ fùjìn	附近
3rd floor	▸ sānlóu	三樓

It's a little far. It's some distance away.

Yǒu diǎr yuǎn, yào zǒu yí duàn lù.

有點兒遠，要走一段路。

How long does it take on foot?

Zǒulù yào duōjiǔ?

走路要多久？

About 10 minutes.

Dàgài shí fēnzhōng.

大概十分鐘。

You are better off taking a bus.

Nǐ zuìhǎo dā chē qù.

你最好搭車去。

Word Bank 22 Vehicles

bicycle	▶ zìxíngchē	自行車
bus	▶ gōngjiāochē	公交車
	▶ gōngchē	公車
long-distance bus	▶ chángtú kèyùn	長途客運
Mass Rapid Transit (MRT)	▶ jiéyùn	捷運
minibus	▶ xiǎo bāshì	小巴士
motorcycle	▶ mótuōchē	摩托車
streetcar	▶ diànchē	電車
subway	▶ dìtiě	地鐵
taxi	▶ chūzūchē	出租車
	▶ jìchéngchē	計程車
train	▶ huǒchē	火車

2 *Taking a Taxi*

Where can I get a taxi, please?

Qǐngwèn, nǎr kěyǐ jiào chē?

請問，哪兒可以叫車？

Please call a cab for me.

Qǐng tì wǒ jiào chē.

請替我叫車。

Do you know this address?

Nǐ zhīdao zhège dìzhǐ ma?

你知道這個地址嗎？

How much is it to the art gallery?

Dào měishùguǎn duōshao qián?

到美術館多少錢？

To the railroad station, please.

Qǐng dào huǒchēzhàn.

請到火車站。

To Zhengyi Road first, and then to Wangfujing Street.

Xiān dào Zhèngyì Lù, zài dào Wángfǔjǐng Dàjiē.

先到正義路，再到王府井大街。

Please open the trunk.

Qǐng kāi yíxià hòuchēxiāng.

請開一下後車廂。

I am in a hurry. Please drive a bit faster.

Wǒ gǎn shíjiān, qǐng kāi kuài yìdiǎr.

我趕時間，請開快一點兒。

Stop here.

Zài zhèr tíngchē.

在這兒停車。

Stop here for a moment.

Zài zhèr tíng yíxià.

在這兒停一下。

Wait for me for 5 minutes.

Děng wǒ wǔ fēnzhōng.

等我五分鐘。

Please turn down the air conditioning.

Qǐng bǎ lěngqì guān xiǎo yìdiǎr.

請把冷氣關小一點兒。

Set the meter?

Zhào biǎo shōu fèi ma?

照表收費嗎？

How much?

Duōshao qián?

多少錢？

Please give me a receipt.

Qǐng gěi wǒ shōujù.

請給我收據。

In large cities such as Beijing, Shanghai, and Taipei, taxis are clean and quick, and you can hail one down with just a wave of the hand. Drivers normally use the meters, so you don't have to worry about being overcharged. In general, the service is pretty good, and some drivers can even speak English. However, in other areas, you need to call to get a taxi and it is necessary to agree on the price before setting out. The best option is to ask staff at the hotel reception desk to give you a hand.

Taking a taxi is one of the best way to cruise the streets in large cities such as Shanghai, Beijing, and Xi'an, though the fares may vary from one city to another.

Most taxi drivers are courteous and trustworthy. It's not a bad idea for you to hire a taxi on a daily basis and have the driver show you around.

TRANSPORTATION

3 Taking the Bus or Subway

Where is the nearest bus stop, please?

Qǐngwèn, zuì jìn de gōngjiāozhàn zài nǎr?
請問，最近的公交站在哪兒？

Are there any buses to the Sogo Department Store, please?

Yǒu méiyǒu dào Tàipíngyáng Bǎihuò de gōngjiāochē?
有沒有到太平洋百貨的公交車？

Do I have to change buses?

Yào bu yào huàn chē?
要不要換車？

Which stop should I get off at?

Wǒ yīnggāi zài nǎ yí zhàn xià chē?
我應該在哪一站下車？

Where do I buy tickets?

Zài nǎr mǎi piào?
在哪兒買票？

How much is the fare?

Piàojià duōshao qián?
票價多少錢？

I need some change.

Wǒ yào huàn língqián.

我要換零錢。

Do I pay when I get on the bus or when I get off the bus?

Shàng chē shōu fèi háishi xià chē shōu fèi?

上車收費還是下車收費？

All tickets are 15 dollars.

Yílǜ shíwǔ kuài qián.

一律十五塊錢。

Where is the subway station, please?

Qǐngwèn, dìtiězhàn zài nǎr?

請問，地鐵站在哪兒？

Does this train go to the zoo?

Zhè bān chē dào dòngwùyuán ma?

這班車到動物園嗎？

When does the next train arrive?

Xià yì bān chē shénme shíhou lái?

下一班車什麼時候來？

There is a train every 10 minutes.

Shí fēnzhōng yì bān chē.

十分鐘一班車。

Excuse me, have we arrived at Fuxingmen Station yet?

Qǐngwèn, Fùxīngmén Zhàn dào le ma?
請問，復興門站到了嗎？

We are almost there.

Kuài dào le.
快到了。

We are not there yet. It's 2 stops away.

Hái méi dào, háiyǒu liǎng zhàn.
還沒到，還有兩站。

You've missed your stop.

Nǐ zuò guò zhàn le.
你坐過站了。

What stop is this?

Zhè shì nǎ yí zhàn?
這是哪一站？

Please remind me when we get to Fuxingmen Station.

Dào Fùxīngmén Zhàn qǐng gàosu wǒ.
到復興門站請告訴我。

What exit should I take for Jinrong Street?

Dào Jīnróng Jiē yào zǒu nǎge chūkǒu?
到金融街要走哪個出口？

4 *Taking the Train*

Is there a train schedule, please?

Qǐngwèn, yǒu méiyǒu huǒchē shíkèbiǎo?

請問，有沒有火車時刻表？

Which window sells tickets to Guangzhou?

Dào Guǎngzhōu de chēpiào zài nǎge chuāngkǒu mǎi?

到廣州的車票在哪個窗口買？

What time is there a train going to Guangzhou tomorrow morning?

Míngtiān zǎoshang dào Guǎngzhōu, yǒu jǐ diǎn de huǒchē?

明天早上到廣州，有幾點的火車？

There is a train going to Guangzhou at 8:30.

Bā diǎn sānshí fēn yǒu yì bān huǒchē dào Guǎngzhōu.

八點三十分有一班火車到廣州。

There are no seats available.

Méiyǒu wèizi le.

沒有位子了。

Are there any seats available tomorrow afternoon?

Míngtiān xiàwǔ hái yǒu wèizi ma?

明天下午還有位子嗎？

I'd like to cancel the reservation and get a refund.

Wǒ yào tuìpiào.

我要退票。

There will be a handling charge of 13 dollars.

Kòu shǒuxùfèi shísān kuài qián.

扣手續費十三塊錢。

On which platform do I catch the train?

Zài dì-jǐ yuètái shàng chē?

在第幾月台上車？

Platform 2.

Zài dì-èr yuètái.

在第二月台。

Is this the train to Guangzhou?

Zhè shì wǎng Guǎngzhōu de huǒchē ma?

這是往廣州的火車嗎？

The train is about to depart.

Huǒchē kuàiyào kāi le.

火車快要開了。

The train has already departed.

Huǒchē yǐjīng kāi zǒu le.

火車已經開走了。

The train is delayed.

Huǒchē wùdiǎn le.

火車誤點了。

The train will be 20 minutes late.

Zhè bān chē yào wǎn èrshí fēnzhōng.

這班車要晚二十分鐘。

Could I sit here?

Wǒ kěyǐ zuò zhège wèizi ma?

我可以坐這個位子嗎？

This seat has already been taken.

Zhège wèizi yǐjīng yǒu rén zuò le.

這個位子已經有人坐了。

Word Bank 23 In a railroad station

additional train	▶ jiāchē	加車
	▶ jiābānchē	加班車
baggage room	▶ jìcúnchù	寄存處
	▶ jìwùchù	寄物處
canceled	▶ tíngshǐ	停駛
carriage number 5	wǔ hào chēxiāng	五號車廂
delayed	▶ wùdiǎn	誤點
dining car	▶ cānchē	餐車
direct train	▶ zhídáchē	直達車
entrance	▶ rùkǒu	入口
exit	▶ chūkǒu	出口

TRANSPORTATION

express train	▶ tèkuàichē	特快車
hall	▶ dàtīng	大廳
hard sleeper	▶ yìngwò	硬臥
information	▶ fúwùtái	服務台
limited train	▶ duìhào lièchē	對號列車
lost-and-found	▶ shīwù zhāolǐngchù	失物 招領處
lowest bunk	▶ xiàpù	下鋪
luggage check-in	▶ tuōyùn xíngli	托運行李
luggage claim	▶ tíqǔ xíngli ▶ tílǐng xíngli	提取行李 提領行李
non-smoking area	▶ fēixīyānqū	非吸煙區
normal train	▶ pǔtōngchē	普通車
one-way ticket	▶ dānchéngpiào	單程票
platform	▶ yuètái	月台
punch ticket	▶ jiǎnpiào	剪票
punctual	▶ zhǔnshí	準時
restroom	▶ wèishēngjiān ▶ xǐshǒujiān	衛生間 洗手間
round-trip ticket	▶ láihuípiào	來回票

TRANSPORTATION

schedule	▶ shíkèbiǎo	時刻表
seat	▶ zuòwèi	座位
shops	▶ xiǎomàidiàn ▶ fànmàibù	小賣店 販賣部
smoking area	▶ xīyānqū	吸煙區
soft sleeper	▶ ruǎnwò	軟臥
stationmaster's office	▶ zhànzhǎngshì	站長室
ticket office	▶ shòupiàochù	售票處
top bunk	▶ shàngpù	上鋪
waiting room	▶ hòuchēshì	候車室

Do You Know? ❾ Travel by train

1. How to buy train tickets:

As in other parts of the world, there are several ways to buy train tickets in this region. For schedules and other details, please visit the following websites:

China: railwaysofchina.com

www.abkk.com/cn/train/search_station.asp

Taiwan: www.railway.gov.tw/e_index.htm

Hong Kong: www.kcrc.com/html/eng

/index.asp

2. Train types:

You have a handful of choices. However, the train types available in China are different from those in Taiwan:

China	
Special Express-w/air-con	*****
Fast Speed-w/air-con	*****
Fast Speed	****
Normal Speed-w/air-con	****
Normal Speed	***

The train has four classes, i.e. hard seat, soft seat, hard sleeper, and soft sleeper.

Taiwan	
Tze-chiang	*****
Chu-kuang	*****
Fu-hsing	****
Ordinary Express	***
Express Train	***
Ordinary Train	**

In Taiwan, four major routes, namely, the Cross-Island Route, the West Line, the East Line, and the South Line, can bring you literally to every corner of the island.

5 By Car

Is this the road to Harbin?

Zhè tiáo lù dào Hā'ěrbīn ma?

這條路到哈爾濱嗎？

Where can I get onto the freeway?

Nǎr kěyǐ shàng gāosù gōnglù?

哪兒可以上高速公路？

Up ahead you will find the freeway tollbooth.

Qiánmian shì gāosù gōnglù shōufèizhàn.

前面是高速公路收費站。

I want to go to Shenyang. Which way should I go?

Wǒ xiǎng dào Shěnyáng, yào zǒu nǎ tiáo lù?

我想到瀋陽，要走哪條路？

Will we pass Dawang Road?

Huì jīngguò Dàwàng Lù ma?

會經過大旺路嗎？

It is rush hour now.

Xiànzài shì jiāotōng gāofēng shíjiān.

現在是交通高峰時間。

There are often traffic jams on this road.

Zhè tiáo lù huì dǔchē.

這條路會堵車。

Which route is closer?

Zǒu nǎ tiáo lù bǐjiào jìn?

走哪條路比較近？

Is it okay to park here?

Zhèr kěyǐ tíngchē ma?

這兒可以停車嗎？

Where can I find a parking lot?

Nǎr yǒu tíngchēchǎng?

哪兒有停車場？

How much is the parking fee per hour?

Tíngchēfèi yí ge xiǎoshí duōshao qián?

停車費一個小時多少錢？

Your car will be towed away if you park here.

Zhèr tíngchē huì bèi tuōdiào.

這兒停車會被拖吊。

Are there any gas stations nearby?

Fùjìn yǒu méiyǒu jiāyóuzhàn?

附近有沒有加油站？

Please fill it up.

Qǐng jiā mǎn.

請加滿。

Please give me 500 dollars worth of gas.

Qǐng jiā wǔbǎi kuài qián qìyóu.

請加五百塊錢汽油。

Lead-free, please.

Jiā wúqiān qìyóu.
加無鉛汽油。

Please wash my car.

Qǐng bāng wǒ xǐ chē.
請幫我洗車。

My car has broken down.

Wǒ de chē huài le.
我的車壞了。 see pp.276-277

Please repair it for me.

Qǐng bāng wǒ xiūlǐ.
請幫我修理。

Do You Know? ⑩ Traffic signs

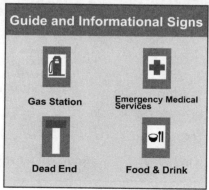

Guide and Informational Signs

Gas Station

Emergency Medical Services

Dead End

Food & Drink

Warning Signs

Right Lane Ends

Steep Uphill Slope

Slippery Road

Railroad Crossing Without Gate

Falling Rocks (L)

Tunnel

Regulatory Signs

停

Stop

停車
檢查

Checkpoint

One Way

Roundabout Traffic Direction

Pedestrians Only

Automobiles Only

Prohibitory Signs

No Bicycle

No Entry

No Automobiles

No Left Turn

No U-Turn

No Temporary Parking

Restriction Signs

Minimum Speed

Maximum Speed

TRANSPORTATION

75

6 Taking a Plane

I want 2 tickets for March 5 to Hong Kong.

Wǒ yào mǎi liǎng zhāng sānyuè wǔ hào dào Xiānggǎng de piào.

我要買兩張三月五號到香港的票。

I want to buy an economy class ticket.

Wǒ yào mǎi jīngjìcāng de piào.

我要買經濟艙的票。

I want a morning flight.

Wǒ yào dā shàngwǔ de bānjī.

我要搭上午的班機。

The morning flight is fully booked. There are seats available on the afternoon flight.

Shàngwǔ kèmǎn le. Xiàwǔ hái yǒu wèizi.

上午客滿了。下午還有位子。

Please let me register your passport details.

Hùzhào qǐng ràng wǒ dēngjì yíxià.

護照請讓我登記一下。

I want a window seat.

Wǒ yào kào chuāng zuòwèi.

我要靠窗座位。

May I pay by credit card?

Kěyǐ shuākǎ ma?
可以刷卡嗎？

Please sign here.

Qǐng zài zhèr qiānmíng.
請在這兒簽名。

Please check in one hour early.

Qǐng nín tíqián yí ge xiǎoshí bàodào.
請您提前一個小時報到。

Word Bank 24 At the ticket office

one-way ticket	▶ dānchéngpiào	單程票
round-trip ticket	▶ láihuípiào	來回票
first class	▶ tóuděngcāng	頭等艙
business class	▶ shāngwùcāng	商務艙
economy class	▶ jīngjìcāng	經濟艙
window seat	▶ kào chuāng zuòwèi	靠窗 座位
aisle seat	▶ kào zǒudào zuòwèi	靠走道 座位
front row	▶ qiánpái	前排
back row	▶ hòupái	後排

TRANSPORTATION

I have booked the ticket online.

Wǒ zài wǎngshang dìngle piào.

我在網上訂了票。

This is my reservation number.

Zhè shì wǒ de dìngpiào hàomǎ.

這是我的訂票號碼。

I have 2 suitcases to check in.

Wǒ yǒu liǎng jiàn xíngli yào tuōyùn.

我有兩件行李要托運。

Your luggage is over the weight limit.

Nín de xíngli chāozhòng le.

您的行李超重了。

Please carry any valuable items with you.

Guìzhòng wùpǐn qǐng suíshēn xiédài.

貴重物品請隨身攜帶。

I'm not carrying any contraband goods with me.

Wǒ méiyǒu jìnpǐn.

我沒有禁品。

This is your boarding pass.

Zhè shì nín de dēngjīpái.

這是您的登機牌。

Please proceed to Gate 3.

Qǐng dào sān hào dēngjīmén.

請到三號登機門。

I'd like to confirm my reservation.

Wǒ yào quèrèn jīwèi.

我要確認機位。

I'd like to cancel my reservation.

Wǒ yào qǔxiāo jīwèi.

我要取消機位。

I missed the flight.

Wǒ méi gǎnshang fēijī.

我沒趕上飛機。

I want to change my flight to tomorrow afternoon at 5:00 p.m.

Wǒ xiǎng gǎi dā míngtiān xiàwǔ wǔ diǎn de fēijī.

我想改搭明天下午五點的飛機。

Where is the baggage claim area?

Zài nǎr tíqǔ xíngli?

在哪兒提取行李？

The flight has been delayed.

Bānjī wùdiǎn le.

班機誤點了。

The flight has been delayed by an hour.

Zhè bān fēijī yào yánhòu yí ge xiǎoshí qǐfēi.

這班飛機要延後一個小時起飛。

We are taking off shortly.

Fēijī jiùyào qǐfēi le.
飛機就要起飛了。

Life jackets are under the seats.

Jiùshēngyī zài zuòwèi dǐxia.
救生衣在座位底下。

Please fasten your seat belt.

Qǐng bǎ ānquándài jì hǎo.
請把安全帶繫好。

Smoking is prohibited.

Jìnzhǐ xīyān.
禁止吸煙。

Please refrain from using your cell phone.

Jìnzhǐ shǐyòng shǒujī.
禁止使用手機。

Please turn off all electronic devices.

Jìnzhǐ shǐyòng diànzǐ chǎnpǐn.
禁止使用電子產品。

I would like to have some juice.

Wǒ yào guǒzhī.
我要果汁。

Please give me a blanket.

Qǐng gěi wǒ máotǎn.
請給我毛毯。

Word Bank 25 Services available on board

beef	▶ niúròu	牛肉
beer	▶ píjiǔ	啤酒
black tea	▶ hóngchá	紅茶
blanket	▶ máotǎn	毛毯
chicken	▶ jīròu	雞肉
coffee	▶ kāfēi	咖啡
cola	▶ kělè	可樂
headset	▶ ěrjī	耳機
juice	▶ guǒzhī	果汁
magazine	▶ zázhì	雜誌
mineral water	▶ kuàngquánshuǐ	礦泉水
newspaper	▶ bàozhǐ	報紙
noodle	▶ miàn	麵
pillow	▶ zhěntou	枕頭
pork	▶ zhūròu	豬肉
rice	▶ fàn	飯
towel	▶ máojīn	毛巾
vegetarian food	▶ sùshí	素食

TRANSPORTATION

May I change seats?

Wǒ kěyǐ huàn wèizi ma?
我可以換位子嗎？

We are now encountering some air turbulence.

Fēijī yùdào qìliú.
飛機遇到氣流。

Please set your table upright.

Qǐng bǎ cānzhuō shōu qilai.
請把餐桌收起來。

Please move your chair to its upright position.

Qǐng bǎ yǐbèi dǎzhí.
請把椅背打直。

We are about to land.

Fēijī jiùyào jiàngluò le.
飛機就要降落了。

Word Bank 26 Signs in an airport

airliner	▶ hángkōng gōngsī	航空公司
airport tax	▶ jīchǎngshuì	機場稅
arrival	▶ rùjìng	入境

baggage claim	▶ tíqǔ xíngli	提取行李
bank	▶ yínháng	銀行
boarding gate	▶ dēngjīmén	登機門
bus stop	▶ gōngjiāozhàn ▶ gōngchēzhàn	公交站 公車站
counter	▶ guìtái	櫃檯
customs	▶ hǎiguān	海關
departure	▶ chūjìng	出境
departure lounge	▶ hòujīshì	候機室
domestic flight	▶ guónèixiàn	國內線
duty-free shop	▶ miǎnshuì shāngdiàn	免稅商店
information	▶ fúwùtái	服務台
inspection line	▶ jiǎncháxiàn	檢查線
insurance	▶ bǎoxiǎn	保險
international flight	▶ guójìxiàn	國際線
lost-and-found	▶ shīwù zhāolǐngchù	失物招領處

TRANSPORTATION

luggage check-in	▶ tuōyùn xíngli	托運行李
nursery	▶ yùyīngshì	育嬰室
restaurant	▶ cāntīng	餐廳
smoking room	▶ xīyānshì	吸煙室
to arrive	▶ dǐdá	抵達
to depart	▶ chūfā	出發
transfer	▶ zhuǎnjī	轉機

7 *Taking a Boat*

I'd like to reserve a ticket to Qingdao.

Wǒ yào yùdìng dào Qīngdǎo de chuánpiào.
我要預訂到青島的船票。

How much is the ticket?

Piàojià duōshao qián?
票價多少錢？

I want a one-way ticket.

Wǒ yào mǎi dānchéngpiào.
我要買單程票。

Are there any tour boats for the Yangtze River and the Three Gorges?

Yǒu méiyǒu Chángjiāng Sānxiá de guānguāngchuán?
有沒有長江三峽的觀光船？

What time does it depart?

Shénme shíhou kāi chuán?
什麼時候開船？

Tomorrow morning at 8 o'clock.

Míngtiān zǎoshang bā diǎn kāi chuán.
明天早上八點開船。

How long does it take?

Yào zuò duōjiǔ?
要坐多久？

It takes 8 hours altogether.

Yígòng bā ge zhōngtóu.
一共八個鐘頭。

Does the fare include lunch?

Chuánpiào bāohán wǔcān ma?
船票包含午餐嗎？

Yes, both lunch and insurance are included in the ticket.

Shì, bāohán wǔcān hé bǎoxiǎn.
是，包含午餐和保險。

Where do I board?

Zài nǎr shàngchuán?
在哪兒上船？

At wharf number 7 just in front.

Qiánmian qī hào mǎtou.
前面七號碼頭。

What time is boarding?

Shénme shíhou dēngchuán?
什麼時候登船？

Boarding starts at 7:00 a.m.

Qī diǎn kāishǐ dēngchuán.

七點開始登船。

May I sit on the deck?

Wǒ kěyǐ zuò zài jiǎbǎn shang ma?

我可以坐在甲板上嗎？

No, you should stay in the cabin.

Bùxíng. Nín yīnggāi zuò zài chuáncāng li.

不行。您應該坐在船艙裡。

I am seasick. Are there any seasickness bags?

Wǒ yùnchuán le, yǒu méiyǒu ǒutùdài?

我暈船了，有沒有嘔吐袋？

Are there life jackets?

Yǒu méiyǒu jiùshēngyī?

有沒有救生衣？

Life jackets are under the seats.

Jiùshēngyī zài zuòwèi dǐxia.

救生衣在座位底下。

Are we going to spend the night on the boat?

Wǒmen zài chuánshang guòyè ma?

我們在船上過夜嗎？

The quality of air in the cabin is not very good.

Chuáncāng li de kōngqì bú tài hǎo.

船艙裡的空氣不太好。

The sea is very calm today.

Jīntiān shuǐmiàn hěn píngjìng.
今天水面很平靜。

The sea is very rough today.

Jīntiān fēnglàng hěn dà.
今天風浪很大。

The trip has been canceled.

Chuánbān qǔxiāo le.
船班取消了。

Word Bank 27 Taking a boat

cabin	▶ chuáncāng	船艙
deck	▶ jiǎbǎn	甲板
life jacket	▶ jiùshēngyī	救生衣
lower deck	▶ xiàcéng	下層
port	▶ gǎngkǒu	港口
seasickness	▶ yùnchuán	暈船
seasickness bag	▶ ǒutùdài	嘔吐袋
seasickness medicine	▶ yùnchuányào	暈船藥
upper deck	▶ shàngcéng	上層
wharf	▶ mǎtou	碼頭

Accommodations

1 *Check in*

What's your name, please?

Qǐngwèn nín de dàmíng shì......?
請問您的大名是……？

My family name is Fisher, and my given name is Peter.

Wǒ xìng Fisher, míng jiào Peter.
我姓 Fisher，名叫 Peter。

I have reserved one single for two days.

Wǒ dìngle liǎng tiān de dānrénfáng.
我訂了兩天的單人房。 ► see p.41

Do you have any rooms?

Hái yǒu kōng fángjiān ma?
還有空房間嗎？

How many days are you staying?

Nín dǎsuàn zhù jǐ tiān?
您打算住幾天？

Three days. I am checking out on March 9.

Sān tiān, wǒ dǎsuàn sānyuè jiǔ hào líkāi.
三天，我打算三月九號離開。

I'm staying one more day.

Wǒ xiǎng zài duō zhù yì tiān.
我想再多住一天。

Is there a bathroom in the room?

Fángjiān li yǒu méiyǒu yùshì?
房間裡有沒有浴室？

I need one extra bed.

Wǒ yào jiā yì zhāng chuáng.
我要加一張床。

Word Bank 28 Room facilities I

English	Pinyin	Chinese
balcony	yángtái	陽台
bathroom	yùshì	浴室
bathtub	yùgāng	浴缸
bed	chuáng	床
carpet	dìtǎn	地毯
chair	yǐzi	椅子
desk	zhuōzi	桌子
hot water	rèshuǐ	熱水
sofa	shāfā	沙發

ACCOMMODATIONS

Could I see the room?

Kěyǐ kànkan fángjiān ma?

可以看看房間嗎？

I'd like a room with a better view.

Wǒ yào jǐngguān hǎo yìdiǎr de fángjiān.

我要景觀好一點兒的房間。

I'd like a room with a mountain view.

Wǒ yào miànshān de fángjiān.

我要面山的房間。

I'd like a room with a sea view.

Wǒ yào miànhǎi de fángjiān.

我要面海的房間。

I'd like a room on the higher levels.

Wǒ yào lóucéng gāo yìdiǎr de fángjiān.

我要樓層高一點兒的房間。

Is a room on the tenth floor good enough for you?

Shí lóu de fángjiān kěyǐ ma?

十樓的房間可以嗎？

I'd like a room with windows.

Wǒ yào yǒu chuānghu de fángjiān.

我要有窗戶的房間。

I'd like a room on the smoking floor.

Wǒ yào xīyān lóucéng de fángjiān.

我要吸煙樓層的房間。

A room on the non-smoking floor would be better.

Jìnyān lóucéng de fángjiān bǐjiào hǎo.

禁煙樓層的房間比較好。

How much is your cheapest room for one day?

Zuì piányi de fángjiān, yì tiān duōshao qián?

最便宜的房間，一天多少錢？

Do I have to pay in advance?

Yào xiān fù qián ma?

要先付錢嗎？

Note 9

Which floor are we on?

It's so easy to talk about floors in Chinese. All you have to do is to place the number before the word "floor (lóu)." For instance, for 20th floor, just say "èrshí lóu."

U.S.A.	Europe	China/Taiwan
basement	cellar	dìxiàshì (地下室)
first floor	ground floor	yì lóu (一樓)
second floor	first floor	èr lóu (二樓)
third floor	second floor	sān lóu (三樓)
lobby	lobby	dàtīng (大廳)

Is there a service charge?

Fúwùfèi wàijiā ma?
服務費外加嗎？

Does that include tax?

Hán shuì ma?
含稅嗎？

Is breakfast included?

Hán zǎocān ma?
含早餐嗎？

Is there a free shuttle service to and forth the airport?

Yǒu dào jīchǎng de miǎnfèi jiēsòng ma?
有到機場的免費接送嗎？

Is there a Chinese restaurant in the hotel?

Fàndiàn li yǒu méiyǒu zhōngcāntīng?
飯店裡有沒有中餐廳？

Do I have free access to the indoor swimming pool?

Kěyǐ miǎnfèi shǐyòng shìnèi yóuyǒngchí ma?
可以免費使用室內游泳池嗎？

Please introduce me some places nearby that are worth visiting.

Qǐng tì wǒ jièshào fùjìn hǎowán de jǐngdiǎn.
請替我介紹附近好玩的景點。

Do you have a city map?

Yǒu méiyǒu shìqū dìtú?

有沒有市區地圖？

Word Bank 29 Hotel facilities

aerobics studio	▶ yùnlǜ jiàoshì	韻律教室
bar	▶ jiǔbā	酒吧
boutique	▶ jīngpǐndiàn	精品店
business center	shāngwù zhōngxīn	商務中心
café	▶ kāfēiguǎn ▶ kāfēitīng	咖啡館 咖啡廳
cafeteria	▶ zìzhù cāntīng	自助餐廳
conference room	▶ huìyìshì	會議室
fitness center	▶ jiànshēnfáng	健身房
Italian restaurant	▶ yìdàlì cāntīng	意大利餐廳
Japanese restaurant	▶ rìběn cāntīng ▶ rìběn liàolǐ diàn	日本餐廳 日本料理店
parking lot	▶ tíngchēchǎng	停車場
salon	▶ měiróngyuàn	美容院
sauna	▶ sāngnáyù ▶ sānwēnnuǎn	桑拿浴 三溫暖

spa	▶ shuǐliáoguǎn	水療館
swimming pool	▶ yóuyǒngchí	游泳池
tennis court	▶ wǎngqiúchǎng	網球場
Western restaurant	▶ xīcāntīng	西餐廳

Please fill out this form.

Qǐng tián zhèi zhāng biǎo.
請填這張表。

Could I see your passport, please?

Qǐng ràng wǒ kànkan nín de hùzhào.
請讓我看看您的護照。

Please sign here.

Qǐng zài zhèli qiānmíng.
請在這裡簽名。

Can I leave my valuables in the safe?

Kěyǐ jìfàng guìzhòng wùpǐn ma?
可以寄放貴重物品嗎？

Where is the emergency exit?

Jǐnjí chūkǒu zài nǎr?
緊急出口在哪兒？

What's the voltage here?

Zhèli de diànyā duōshao?

這裡的電壓多少？

Please give me my breakfast coupon.

Qǐng gěi wǒ zǎocānquàn.

請給我早餐券。

What time is the breakfast?

Jǐ diǎn kāishǐ gōngyìng zǎocān?

幾點開始供應早餐？

What time should I check out?

Jǐ diǎn tuìfáng?

幾點退房？

Before 12:00 noon.

Zhōngwǔ shí'èr diǎn yǐqián.

中午十二點以前。 ▶ see p.33

This is your key.

Zhè shì nín de yàoshi.

這是您的鑰匙。

This way, please.

Qǐng gēn wǒ lái.

請跟我來。

Please have someone carry my baggage.

Qǐng zhǎo rén bāng wǒ tí xíngli.

請找人幫我提行李。

Do You Know? ⑪ About tips

Generally speaking, tips are not expected in the more economic lodging facilities, where service charges and tips are normally included in the price. However, if you are staying in a top-end hotel, you are supposed to tip the bellman, room service provider, and the housekeeping personnel.

Notes

ACCOMMODATIONS

2 *Complaints about the Room*

My bags haven't been sent up yet.

Wǒ de xíngli hái méi sònglai.

我的行李還沒送來。

I forgot my room number.

Wǒ wàngle fángjiān hàomǎ.

我忘了房間號碼。

I've lost my key.

Wǒ de yàoshi bújiàn le.

我的鑰匙不見了。

I left my key in my room.

Wǒ bǎ yàoshi fàngzài fángjiān li le.

我把鑰匙放在房間裡了。

My room is too cold.

Wǒ de fángjiān tài lěng le.

我的房間太冷了。

I want a warmer room.

Wǒ yào nuǎnhuo yìdiǎr de fángjiān.

我要暖和一點兒的房間。

My bed sheet is dirty.

Wǒ de chuángdān zāng le.

我的床單髒了。

It's dusty in my room.

Fángjiān li dōushì huīchén.

房間裡都是灰塵。

Word Bank 30 Room conditions (unpleasant)

dark	▶ àn	暗
dirty	▶ zāng	髒
hot	▶ rè	熱
moist/wet	▶ shī	濕
noisy	▶ chǎo	吵
small	▶ xiǎo	小

Word Bank 31 Room conditions (pleasant)

bright	▶ liàng	亮
clean	▶ gānjìng	乾淨
nice and cool	▶ liángkuai	涼快
dry	▶ gānshuǎng	乾爽
quiet	▶ ānjìng	安靜
big	▶ dà	大

Please send someone to clean up the room.

Qǐng pài rén lái dǎsǎo fángjiān.

請派人來打掃房間。

The air conditioner does not work.

Kōngtiáo huài le.

空調壞了。

I can't use the telephone.

Diànhuà bù néng yòng.

電話不能用。

The hot water isn't hot enough.

Rèshuǐ bú gòu rè.

熱水不夠熱。

The room next door is noisy.

Gébì fángjiān hěn chǎo.

隔壁房間很吵。

My camera was stolen from my room.

Wǒ fàngzài fángjiān li de xiàngjī bèi tōu le.

我放在房間裡的相機被偷了。

Please send someone to see to it.

Qǐng pài rén lái chǔlǐ yíxià.

請派人來處理一下。

I want to change rooms.

Wǒ yào huàn fángjiān.

我要換房間。

Word Bank 32 Room facilities II

air conditioner	▶ kōngtiáo	空調
curtain	▶ chuānglián	窗簾
electric jug	▶ diànshuǐhú	電水壺
fan	▶ diànshàn	電扇
faucet	▶ shuǐlóngtóu	水龍頭
heater	▶ nuǎnqì	暖氣
jacuzzi	▶ ànmóyùgāng	按摩浴缸
lamp	▶ táidēng	檯燈
light	▶ diàndēng	電燈
lock	▶ suǒ	鎖
pay TV	▶ fùfèi diànshì	付費電視
refrigerator	▶ bīngxiāng	冰箱
safe	▶ bǎoxiǎnxiāng	保險箱
satellite TV	▶ wèixīng diànshì	衛星電視
shower head	▶ pēntóu ▶ liánpéngtóu	噴頭 蓮蓬頭
socket	▶ chāzuò	插座
telephone	▶ diànhuà	電話
television	▶ diànshì	電視
toilet	▶ mǎtǒng	馬桶
window	▶ chuānghu	窗戶

ACCOMMODATIONS

3 *In the Room*

This is Room 711.

Zhèr shì qī yāo yāo hào fáng.
這兒是 711 號房。

Please wake me up at 7:00 tomorrow morning.

Míngtiān zǎoshang qī diǎn qǐng jiào wǒ qǐchuáng.
明天早上七點請叫我起床。

Please give me some hot drinking water.

Qǐng gěi wǒ rè kāishuǐ.
請給我熱開水。

Please change the sheets.

Qǐng huàn chuángdān.
請換床單。

Please bring me one Chinese breakfast.

Qǐng gěi wǒ yí fèn zhōngshì zǎocān.
請給我一份中式早餐。

I'd like to have a Continental breakfast.

Wǒ yào yí fèn xīshì zǎocān.
我要一份西式早餐。

I'd like these clothes cleaned.

Wǒ yào sòngxǐ zhèixiē yīfu.
我要送洗這些衣服。

Please have this skirt ironed.

Qǐng bāng wǒ tàng zhèi tiáo qúnzi.
請幫我燙這條裙子。

Word Bank 33 Things you might need

ashtray	▶ yānhuīgāng	煙灰缸
bath lotion	▶ mùyùlù	沐浴露
	▶ mùyùrǔ	沐浴乳
bath towel	▶ yùjīn	浴巾
blanket	▶ tǎnzi	毯子
coffee mate	▶ kāfēi bànlǚ	咖啡伴侶
	▶ nǎijīng	奶精
cold drinking water	▶ liáng kāishuǐ	涼開水
	▶ lěng kāishuǐ	冷開水
comb	▶ shūzi	梳子
hair dryer	▶ diànchuīfēng	電吹風
	▶ chuīfēngjī	吹風機
hanger	▶ yījià	衣架
hot drinking water	▶ rè kāishuǐ	熱開水
ice cube	▶ bīngkuài	冰塊

instant coffee	▶ sùróng kāfēi ▶ jíróng kāfēi	速溶咖啡 即溶咖啡
mineral water	▶ kuàngquán shuǐ	礦泉水
mirror	▶ jìngzi	鏡子
newspaper	▶ bàozhǐ	報紙
pillow	▶ zhěntou	枕頭
razor	▶ tìxūdāo ▶ guāhúdāo	剃鬚刀 刮鬍刀
rinse	▶ rùnfàlù ▶ rùnsījīng	潤髮露 潤絲精
sewing kit	▶ zhēnxiànbāo	針線包
shampoo	▶ xǐfàlù ▶ xǐfǎjīng	洗髮露 洗髮精
slippers	▶ tuōxié	拖鞋
soap	▶ féizào	肥皂
sugar	▶ táng	糖
tea bags	▶ chábāo	茶包
toilet paper	▶ wèishēngzhǐ	衛生紙
toothbrush	▶ yáshuā	牙刷
toothpaste	▶ yágāo	牙膏

ACCOMMODATIONS

This shirt needs dry cleaning.

Zhèi jiàn chènshān xūyào gānxǐ.

這件襯衫需要乾洗。

Please charge it to my room.

Qǐng bǎ fèiyong suàndào wǒ de fángzhàng.

請把費用算到我的房賬。

Can I have them back by tonight?

Jīntiān wǎnshang kěyǐ xǐhǎo ma?

今天晚上可以洗好嗎？

This is not mine.

Zhèi jiàn bú shì wǒ de.

這件不是我的。

There is one piece missing.

Wǒ shǎole yí jiàn yīfu.

我少了一件衣服。

Is my laundry ready?

Yīfu xǐhǎo le ma?

衣服洗好了嗎？

Please deliver to my room asap.

Qǐng jǐnkuài sòngdào wǒ de fángjiān lái.

請儘快送到我的房間來。

Word Bank 34 Laundry list

blouse	▶ nǚchènshān	女襯衫
coat	▶ dàyī	大衣
dress	▶ xīzhuāng ▶ yángzhuāng	西裝 洋裝
jacket	▶ wàitào	外套
pants	▶ kùzi	褲子
scarf	▶ wéijīn	圍巾
shirt	▶ chènshān	襯衫
sweater	▶ máoyī	毛衣
T-shirt	▶ T-xùshān ▶ T-xù	T恤衫 T恤

4 *Check out*

I'd like to check out now.

Wǒ yào tuìfáng.
我要退房。

I'm leaving tomorrow morning.

Wǒ dǎsuàn míngtiān zǎoshang tuìfáng.
我打算明天早上退房。

I am paying by cash.

Wǒ yào fùxiàn.
我要付現。

I am paying by credit card.

Wǒ yào shuākǎ.
我要刷卡。

I'm in a hurry.

Wǒ gǎn shíjiān.
我趕時間。

I want to take a look at my bill.

Wǒ xiǎng kàn yíxià zhàngdān.
我想看一下賬單。

What's this for?

Zhè shì shénme fèiyong?
這是什麼費用？

It is the charge for the pay TV.

Zhè shì fùfèi diànshì de fèiyong.

這是付費電視的費用。

I had a beer.

Wǒ hēle yì píng píjiǔ.

我喝了一瓶啤酒。

I didn't make any international phone calls.

Wǒ méi dǎ guójì diànhuà.

我沒打國際電話。

I made two long-distance calls.

Wǒ dǎle liǎng tōng chángtú diànhuà.

我打了兩通長途電話。

I never called room service.

Wǒ méi jiào kèfáng fúwù.

我沒叫客房服務。

Please check the bill again.

Qǐng chóngxīn jiǎnchá zhàngdān.

請重新檢查賬單。

Please give me the bill.

Qǐng gěi wǒ zhàngdān.

請給我賬單。

Please give me an invoice.

Qǐng gěi wǒ fāpiào.

請給我發票。

Please give me a receipt.

Qǐng gěi wǒ shōujù.
請給我收據。

I'd like my valuables from the safe.

Wǒ xiǎng náhui guìzhòng wùpǐn.
我想拿回貴重物品。

Please call me a taxi.

Qǐng bāng wǒ jiào chūzūchē.
請幫我叫出租車。

I am going to the railroad station.

Wǒ yào qù huǒchēzhàn.
我要去火車站。

Please drive me to the airport.

Qǐng sòng wǒ dào jīchǎng.
請送我到機場。

Please ask the porter to carry my bags.

Qǐng xínglǐyuán bāng wǒ tí xíngli.
請行李員幫我提行李。

May I leave my bags here till 5:00 p.m.?

Wǒ wǔ diǎn huílai ná xíngli, kěyǐ ma?
我五點回來拿行李，可以嗎？

I left some stuff in my room.

Wǒ de dōngxi wàngle ná.
我的東西忘了拿。

Eating

1 Entering a Restaurant

Welcome. How many in your party, please?

Huānyíng guānglín, qǐngwèn jǐ wèi?
歡迎光臨，請問幾位？

Two.

Liǎng wèi.
兩位。

One more person is coming later.

Hái yǒu yí wèi wǎn diǎr dào.
還有一位晚點兒到。

Are there any tables free?

Yǒu wèizi ma?
有位子嗎？

You'll have to wait a little while.

Nín děi shāo děng yíxià.
您得稍等一下。

How long?

Děi děng duōjiǔ?
得等多久？

About 20 minutes.

Dàgài èrshí fēnzhōng.
大概二十分鐘。

All right. We'll wait.

Hǎo ba! Wǒmen děng yíhuìr.

好吧！我們等一會兒。

We'll try another time.

Wǒmen xiàcì zài lái.

我們下次再來。

Sorry, all the tables are occupied.

Hěn bàoqiàn, kèmǎn le.

很抱歉，客滿了。

Did you make a reservation?

Nín dìngwèi le ma?

您訂位了嗎？

I have a reservation. My name is Peter Fisher.

Wǒ yǐjīng dìngwèi le, wǒ jiào Peter Fisher.

我已經訂位了，我叫 Peter Fisher。

I reserved a table for two.

Wǒ dìngle liǎng ge rén de wèizi.

我訂了兩個人的位子。

I reserved a room.

Wǒ dìngle yì jiān bāoxiāng.

我訂了一間包廂。

This way, please, Mr. Fisher.

Fisher xiānsheng, zhèbiān qǐng.

Fisher 先生，這邊請。

Please sit down.

Qǐng zuò.
請坐。

I'd like a table by the window.

Wǒ yào kào chuāng de wèizi.
我要靠窗的位子。

I'd like a quiet table.

Wǒ yào ānjìng de wèizi.
我要安靜的位子。

I'd like a table in the smoking area.

Wǒ yào xīyānqū de wèizi.
我要吸煙區的位子。

I'd like to move to a different table.

Wǒ yào huàn yí ge wèizi.
我要換一個位子。

Are there more tables upstairs?

Lóu shang hái yǒu wèizi ma?
樓上還有位子嗎？

Can I sit outside?

Wǒ kěyǐ zuò wàimian ma?
我可以坐外面嗎？

When do you close?

Nǐmen yíngyè dào jǐ diǎn?
你們營業到幾點？

2 *Ordering Food*

Menu, please.

Qǐng gěi wǒ càidān.
請給我菜單。

Do you have an English menu?

Yǒu méiyǒu Yīngwén càidān?
有沒有英文菜單？

This is the menu. What would you like to order?

Zhè shì càidān, nín yào diǎn shénme?
這是菜單，您要點什麼？

I'll order later when my friends are here.

Wǒ děng péngyou, xiān bù diǎncài.
我等朋友，先不點菜。

What do you recommend?

Yǒu shénme hǎochī de?
有什麼好吃的？

Do you have any local dishes?

Yǒu méiyǒu shénme dìfāng míngcài?
有沒有什麼地方名菜？

Do you have any combination sets?

Yǒu méiyǒu hécài?
有沒有合菜？

What's your specialty?

Nǐmen de zhāopáicài shì shénme?

你們的招牌菜是什麼？

Do You Know? ⑫ Round table culture

Chinese people love eating and they do know how to eat. For the Chinese people, cooking is an art. Cook chop food, slice food and do whatever needed to prepare it in the kitchen, so when the dishes are served, they are ready for you to enjoy. Leave your knives and forks in the kitchen, so to speak. Chinese people are all expert chopsticks users, but using chopsticks is often a challenge for foreigners. Don't worry, because cordial and friendly Chinese servers will normally bring you knives and forks.

As eating is such an occasion, the dining table is often the center of social life. You will find that Chinese people like to gather around a round table, serving themselves with delicious food and talking loudly. Everything from family life to world news can be topics. So if, when stepping into a luxurious Chinese restaurant, you find yourself enveloped by loud voices, you know you are about to experience a primary scene of Chinese life.

Sweet-and-sour fish is good.

Tángcùyú búcuò.

糖醋魚不錯。

One sweet-and-sour fish, please.

Lái yí ge tángcùyú.

來一個糖醋魚。

Anything else?

Hái yào shénme?

還要什麼？

One tofu soup, please.

Zài lái yí ge dòufutāng.

再來一個豆腐湯。

Do you have baked egg with prawns?

Nǐmen yǒu méiyǒu xiārén-hōngdàn?

你們有沒有蝦仁烘蛋？

Give me a bowl of rice, please.

Gěi wǒ yì wǎn fàn.

給我一碗飯。

Are there any organ meats in this dish?

Zhè dào cài yǒu méiyǒu nèizàng?

這道菜有沒有內臟？

I am a vegetarian; I don't eat meat.

Wǒ chī sù. Wǒ bù chī ròu.

我吃素。我不吃肉。

What is in this dish?

Zhè dào cài shì shénme zuò de?

這道菜是什麼做的？

This is a chicken dish.

Zhè dào cài shì jīròu zuò de.

這道菜是雞肉做的。

Is this dish spicy?

Zhè dào cài là bu là?

這道菜辣不辣？

I'd like to have it real spicy.

Wǒ yào là yìdiǎr.

我要辣一點兒。

Not too salty.

Búyào tài xián.

不要太鹹。

Not too oily.

Búyào tài yóu.

不要太油。

Please do not add MSG.

Búyào fàng wèijīng.

不要放味精。

(Point to the menu) I would like this.

Wǒ yào diǎn zhèige.

我要點這個。

The same for me.

Wǒ diǎn hé tā yíyàng de.
我點和他一樣的。

I'd like to have some side dishes.

Gěi wǒ lái jǐ pán xiǎocài.
給我來幾盤小菜。

Anything else?

Hái xūyào biéde ma?
還需要別的嗎?

That's enough. Thank you.

Gòu le. Xièxie.
夠了。謝謝。

I will let you know later if we need some more dishes.

Rúguǒ bú gòu, děng yíxià zài diǎn.
如果不夠,等一下再點。

Please settle the bill first.

Qǐng xiān fù kuǎn.
請先付款。

I would like to change my order.

Wǒ xiǎng gǎi diǎn biéde cài.
我想改點別的菜。

I'd like to cancel this order.

Zhè dào cài búyào le.
這道菜不要了。

I'd like to have one more vegetable.

Wǒ xiǎng jiādiǎn yí dào shūcài.
我想加點一道蔬菜。

Take out, please.

Wǒ yào wàidài.
我要外帶。

Word Bank 35 World cuisine

Chinese food	▶ zhōngguócài	中國菜
French food	▶ fǎguócài	法國菜
German food	▶ déguócài	德國菜
Greek food	▶ xīlàcài	希臘菜
Indian food	▶ yìndùcài	印度菜
Italian food	▶ yìdàlìcài	意大利菜
Japanese food	▶ rìběncài	日本菜
Korean food	▶ hánguócài	韓國菜
Mexican food	▶ mòxīgēcài	墨西哥菜
Thai food	▶ tàiguócài	泰國菜

⭐ Please see p.284 for **Menu**.

Please have this packed.

Qǐng tì wǒ bāo qilai.

請替我包起來。

I don't know how to use chopsticks.

Wǒ bú huì yòng kuàizi.

我不會用筷子。

Please give me a knife and fork.

Qǐng gěi wǒ dāochā.

請給我刀叉。

Please give me one more plate.

Qǐng zài gěi wǒ yí ge pánzi.

請再給我一個盤子。

Do You Know? ⑬ The art of Chinese food

Chinese cuisine is an art itself. Food is prepared in many ways. For instance, dishes such as fried rice with scrambled egg is prepared by stir fry, while stewed beef is, of course, stewed. Very often, dumplings, such as small steamed buns, are steamed, but as you may know, boiled dumplings are prepared in boiling water, while the very popular snack, "xiánsūjī," or salted crispy chicken, is deep fried. As for the famous Beijing duck, I guess you know that it is roasted. Different methods of cooking give the same food different looks and tastes.

EATING

121

3 Ordering Drinks

What would you like to drink?

Nín xiǎng hē diǎnr shénme?

您想喝點兒什麼？

Do you have any famous Chinese liquors?

Yǒu méiyǒu zhōngguó míngjiǔ?

有沒有中國名酒？

What's the alcohol percentage?

Jiǔjīngdù yǒu duōshao?

酒精度有多少？

I'd like to have one beer.

Wǒ yào yì bēi píjiǔ.

我要一杯啤酒。

Would you like it in a bottle or in a can?

Nín yào píngzhuāng de háishi guànzhuāng de?

您要瓶裝的還是罐裝的？

A cup of coffee, without sugar, please.

Yì bēi kāfēi, búyào fàng táng.

一杯咖啡，不要放糖。

Hot or cold?

Nín yào rè de háishi bīng de?
您要熱的還是冰的？

Lukewarm, please.

Wǒ yào wēn de.
我要溫的。

Give me a packet of sugar, please.

Gěi wǒ tángbāo.
給我糖包。

Do you have any juice?

Yǒu méiyǒu guǒzhī?
有沒有果汁？

Please give me a straw.

Gěi wǒ yì gēn xīguǎn.
給我一根吸管。

One more, please.

Zài lái yì bēi.
再來一杯。

Please add some ice cubes to this.

Wǒ yào jiā bīngkuài.
我要加冰塊。

Just water will be fine.

Gěi wǒ yì bēi shuǐ jiù xíng le.
給我一杯水就行了。

4 Settling the Bill

Bill, please.

Mǎidān.
買單。

Where should I pay?

Zài nǎli fù qián?
在哪裡付錢？

How much is the total?

Yígòng duōshao qián?
一共多少錢？

Is the service charge included?

Zhè fèiyong bāokuò fúwùfèi ma?
這費用包括服務費嗎？

I'll take care of the bill.

Wǒ qǐngkè.
我請客。

We'd like to pay separately.

Wǒmen gè fù gè de.
我們各付各的。

Can I pay by credit card?

Kěyǐ shuākǎ ma?
可以刷卡嗎？

Here is $700. Keep the change.

Gěi nǐ qībǎi kuài qián, búyòng zhǎo le.

給你七百塊錢，不用找了。

This bill doesn't look right.

Zhàngdān hǎoxiàng yǒu wèntí.

賬單好像有問題。

Please double check.

Qǐng nǐ zài suàn yí cì.

請你再算一次。

I think you gave me the wrong change.

Nǐ zhǎocuò qián le.

你找錯錢了。

Please give me a receipt.

Qǐng nǐ kāi yì zhāng shōujù.

請你開一張收據。

I enjoyed my meal.

Nǐmen de cài hěn hǎochī.

你們的菜很好吃。

Do You Know? 14 Tipping in a restaurant

Most high-end eateries include a 10% service charge in their bills, so customers are not obliged to leave a tip. As for other restaurants and snack shops, there is no service charge and tips are not expected.

5 *Complaints in a Restaurant*

This plate is dirty.

Zhège pánzi zāng le.

這個盤子髒了。

I'd like to have another one.

Wǒ yào huàn yí ge.

我要換一個。

This dish is undercooked.

Zhè dào cài méi zhǔ shóu.

這道菜沒煮熟。

This dish smells strange.

Zhè dào cài wén qilai guàiguài de.

這道菜聞起來怪怪的。

I did not order this.

Wǒ méi diǎn zhè dào cài.

我沒點這道菜。

It's cold here.

Zhèli tài lěng le.

這裡太冷了。

It's noisy here.

Zhèli tài chǎo le.

這裡太吵了。

It's too crowded here.

Zhège wèizi tài xiǎo le.
這個位子太小了。

Please clean up the table.

Qǐng nǐ qīnglǐ yíxià zhuōmiàn.
請你清理一下桌面。

The dishes are coming too slowly.

Nǐmen shàng cài tài màn le.
你們上菜太慢了。

I've been waiting for 30 minutes.

Wǒ yǐjīng děngle sānshí fēnzhōng.
我已經等了三十分鐘。

I ordered two beers, but we only got one.

Wǒ jiàole liǎng bēi píjiǔ, zhǐ láile yì bēi.
我叫了兩杯啤酒，只來了一杯。

The bread is moldy.

Zhège miànbāo fāméi le.
這個麵包發霉了。

This milk has passed the expiration date.

Zhège niúnǎi guòqī le.
這個牛奶過期了。

This bottle of wine is not labeled with the right year.

Zhè píng jiǔ de niánfèn búduì.
這瓶酒的年份不對。

It tastes odd to me.

Wǒ chī bú guàn zhège.

我吃不慣這個。

Word Bank 36 Tableware

bowl	▶ wǎn	碗
can opener	▶ kāipíngqì	開瓶器
chopsticks	▶ kuàizi	筷子
fork	▶ chāzi	叉子
glass	▶ bōlibēi	玻璃杯
knife	▶ dāozi	刀子
napkin	▶ cānjīn	餐巾
plate	▶ pánzi	盤子
small plate	▶ xiǎo diézi	小碟子
soup ladle	▶ tāngsháo	湯勺
tea cup	▶ chábēi	茶杯
teaspoon	▶ xiǎo tāngchí	小湯匙
tissue paper	▶ miànzhǐ	面紙
towel	▶ máojīn	毛巾
wine glass	▶ jiǔbēi	酒杯

EATING

Tour

1 Travel Itinerary

Which tours do you offer?

Yǒu nǎxiē lǚyóutuán?

有哪些旅遊團？

Which tour is the most popular one?

Nǎ yí ge lǚyóutuán zuì shòu huānyíng?

哪一個旅遊團最受歡迎？

Are there any tours to Taroko Gorge tomorrow?

Míngtiān yǒu méiyǒu dào Tàilǔgé de lǚyóutuán?

明天有沒有到太魯閣的旅遊團？

I'd like to join this tour.

Wǒ xiǎng cānjiā zhèige tuán.

我想參加這個團。

Which places will we visit?

Huì cānguān nǎixiē dìfang?

會參觀哪些地方？

Are there any other tours?

Hái yǒu biéde lǚyóutuán ma?

還有別的旅遊團嗎？

Do you have a half-day tour?

Yǒu bànrìyóu de tuán ma?
有半日遊的團嗎？

How much does it cost?

Fèiyong duōshao qián?
費用多少錢？

Three hundred and fifty dollars per person.

Yí ge rén sānbǎi wǔshí kuài.
一個人三百五十塊。

Can I get a discount with a student ID card?

Píng xuéshēngzhèng yǒu yōudài ma?
憑學生證有優待嗎？

Are there any extra charges?

Yǒu méiyǒu éwài de fèiyong?
有沒有額外的費用？

Is insurance included?

Hán bǎoxiǎn ma?
含保險嗎？

Are lunch and the entrance fee included?

Hán wǔcān gēn ménpiào ma?
含午餐跟門票嗎？

I'd like to cancel my place on this tour.

Wǒ yào qǔxiāo zhèige lǚyóutuán.
我要取消這個旅遊團。

Can I get a refund?

Kěyǐ tuì fèi ma?

可以退費嗎？

We can only refund 80% of the cost.

Zhǐ néng tuì bǎi fēn zhī bāshí.

只能退百分之八十。

Where should I meet up with you?

Zài nǎr jíhé?

在哪兒集合？

When do we set out?

Shénme shíhou chūfā?

什麼時候出發？

When do we come back?

Shénme shíhou huílai?

什麼時候回來？

How long will we stay at the museum?

Huì zài bówùguǎn tíngliú duōjiǔ?

會在博物館停留多久？

Will we have any free time?

Yǒu méiyǒu zìyóu huódòng de shíjiān?

有沒有自由活動的時間？

What do I need to take?

Wǒ yào dài shénme dōngxi?

我要帶什麼東西？

Is there an English-speaking guide?

Yǒu méiyǒu Yīngyǔ dǎoyóu?

有沒有英語導遊？

Do you have an English map?

Yǒu méiyǒu Yīngwén dìtú?

有沒有英文地圖？

Could you pick me up at the hotel?

Kěyǐ dào lǚguǎn jiē wǒ ma?

可以到旅館接我嗎？

Could you take me back to the hotel?

Kěyǐ sòng wǒ huí lǚguǎn ma?

可以送我回旅館嗎？

Word Bank 37 Items you will need while traveling

bug repellent	qūchóngjì	驅蟲劑
camera	zhàoxiàngjī	照相機
camera film	dǐpiàn	底片
change	língqián	零錢
flashlight	shǒudiàntǒng	手電筒
hat	màozi	帽子
map	dìtú	地圖
passport	hùzhào	護照
safety glasses	hùmùjìng	護目鏡
warm clothes	yùhán yīwù	禦寒衣物

2 *Cultural Activities*

I'd like to go to a concert.

Wǒ xiǎng qù tīng yīnyuèhuì.

我想去聽音樂會。

I'd like to go to a show.

Wǒ xiǎng qù kàn biǎoyǎn.

我想去看表演。

Please give me this week's program.

Qǐng gěi wǒ zhèige xīngqī de jiémùdān.

請給我這個星期的節目單。

What's on tonight?

Jīntiān wǎnshang yǒu shénme jiémù?

今天晚上有什麼節目？

Is there any Beijing Opera on tonight?

Jīntiān wǎnshang yǒu jīngjù biǎoyǎn ma?

今天晚上有京劇表演嗎？

Do you have an English brochure?

Yǒu méiyǒu Yīngwén jiémùdān?

有沒有英文節目單？

What time does the show start?

Jǐ diǎn kāishǐ?

幾點開始？

Word Bank 38 Popular shows

acrobatic performance	▶ zájì	雜技
ballet	▶ bālěiwǔ	芭蕾舞
Beijing Opera	▶ jīngjù	京劇
cross talk	▶ xiàngsheng	相聲
erhu recital	▶ èrhú yǎnzòu	二胡演奏
flute recital	▶ dízi yǎnzòu	笛子演奏
folk dance	▶ mínzú wǔdǎo	民族舞蹈
folk music	▶ mínyáo	民謠
Kun Opera	▶ kūnqǔ	崑曲
martial arts performance	▶ wǔshù	武術
orchestra	▶ guǎnxiányuè	管弦樂
percussion	▶ dǎjīyuè	打擊樂
piano recital	▶ gāngqín yǎnzòu	鋼琴演奏
pipa recital	▶ pípa yǎnzòu	琵琶演奏
pop concert	▶ yǎnchànghuì	演唱會
puppet show	▶ mù'ǒuxì ▶ ǒuxì	木偶戲 偶戲
symphony	▶ jiāoxiǎngyuè	交響樂
zither recital	▶ gǔzhēng yǎnzòu	古箏演奏

How long is the show?

Jiémù duōcháng?

節目多長？

Are there any seats left?

Hái yǒu wèizi ma?

還有位子嗎？

I'd like to buy a ticket for tonight's show.

Wǒ yào mǎi jīntiān wǎnshang de piào.

我要買今天晚上的票。

Can I buy tickets at the door?

Kěyǐ xiànchǎng mǎi piào ma?

可以現場買票嗎？

How much is a ticket?

Piàojià duōshao qián?

票價多少錢？

I'd like 2 one-hundred-dollar tickets.

Wǒ yào mǎi liǎng zhāng yìbǎi yuán de piào.

我要買兩張一百元的票。

Is there an intermission?

Yǒu méiyǒu zhōngchǎng xiūxi shíjiān?

有沒有中場休息時間？

Is the show in Chinese?

Yǎnyuán yòng Zhōngwén biǎoyǎn ma?

演員用中文表演嗎？

Are there English subtitles?

Yǒu méiyǒu Yīngwén zìmù?
有沒有英文字幕？

There are English subtitles at the side of the stage.

Wǔtái pángbiān yǒu Yīngwén zìmù.
舞台旁邊有英文字幕。

Are there any art galleries nearby?

Fùjìn yǒu méiyǒu měishùguǎn?
附近有沒有美術館？

Could you take me there?

Nǐ kěyǐ dài wǒ qù ma?
你可以帶我去嗎？

When does it open?

Zhèr jǐ diǎn kāimén?
這兒幾點開門？

When does it close?

Zhèr jǐ diǎn guānmén?
這兒幾點關門？

Where's the ticket office?

Shòupiàochù zài nǎr?
售票處在哪兒？

Is admission free?

Miǎnfèi rùchǎng ma?
免費入場嗎？

Word Bank 39 Places worth visiting

amusement park	▶ yóulèyuán	遊樂園
art gallery	▶ měishùguǎn	美術館
beach	▶ hǎitān	海灘
church	▶ jiàotáng	教堂
department store	▶ bǎihuò gōngsī	百貨公司
exhibition	▶ zhǎnlǎnhuì	展覽會
fair	▶ jíshì ▶ shìjí	集市 市集
historical site	▶ gǔjì	古蹟
hot spring	▶ wēnquán	溫泉
market	▶ shìchǎng	市場
movie theater	▶ diànyǐngyuàn	電影院
museum	▶ bówùguǎn	博物館
night market	▶ yèshì	夜市
opera house	▶ gējùyuàn	歌劇院
park	▶ gōngyuán	公園
scenic area	▶ fēngjǐngqū	風景區
supermarket	▶ chāojí shìchǎng	超級市場
temple	▶ sìmiào	寺廟

Which exhibition is being shown today?

Jīntiān zhǎnlǎn shénme?

今天展覽什麼？

Where does it start?

Cóng nǎr kāishǐ cānguān?

從哪兒開始參觀？

Are there English guides?

Yǒu Yīngwén jiěshuō ma?

有英文解說嗎？

Word Bank 40 Words you may see while visiting

entrance	rùkǒu	入口
exit	chūkǒu	出口
...is forbidden	jìnzhǐ......	禁止……
please don't...	qǐng wù......	請勿……
restroom	wèishēngjiān	衛生間
	xǐshǒujiān	洗手間
shop	xiǎomàidiàn	小賣店
	fànmàichù	販賣處
souvenir	jìniànpǐn	紀念品
ticket office	shòupiàochù	售票處
toilet	cèsuǒ	廁所
welcome	huānyíng	歡迎

3 *Folk Activities*

What is today's festival for?

Jīntiān shì shénme jiérì?
今天是什麼節日？

What events will there be?

Yǒu shénme huódòng?
有什麼活動？

Are there any local customs?

Yǒu shénme dìfāng xísú ma?
有什麼地方習俗嗎？

Is there a folk performance?

Yǒu mínsú biǎoyǎn ma?
有民俗表演嗎？

Are there any traditional specialties?

Yǒu shénme chuántǒng shíwù ma?
有什麼傳統食物嗎？

Are there any taboos?

Yǒu shénme jìnjì ma?
有什麼禁忌嗎？

Do you wear traditional costumes?

Yào chuān chuántǒng fúzhuāng ma?
要穿傳統服裝嗎？

The Must-Eats for Certain Folk Festivals

Chinese New Year

Hot Pot 火鍋 huǒguō

Family members gather around a hot pot, and prepare their food in the pot. Hot pot is a symbol of unification and sharing.

Boiled Pork Dumpling 水餃 shuǐjiǎo

Minced meat is wrapped in the dough and made into the shape of a golden ingot. This dumpling cooked in boiling water is therefore viewed as a symbol of wealth. If you find a coin in the dumpling you eat, then you will certainly have a very prosperous, happy new year.

Glutinous Rice Cake 年糕 niángāo

The Chinese people do have cakes on New Year's Day except that their cakes are steamed instead of baked. Eating cake (gāo 糕), pronounced the same as "high" (gāo 高), is a symbol of going higher and higher, or becoming more and more prosperous in the coming new year.

Dragon Boat Festival

Glutinous Rice Dumpling 粽子 zòngzi

This triangular glutinous rice dumpling is wrapped with bamboo leaves and filled with all kinds of stuffing. Legend has it that a poet who was also a patriot drowned himself in a river. To distract the fish from his dead body, people threw rice dumplings into the river and boated down the river to chase the fish away. In memory of the poet, people eat this dumpling every year since then.

Realgar Wine 雄黃酒 xiónghuángjiǔ

Realgar wine is made of a kind of herb that is part of the Chinese herb doctors' repertoire. It is believed that during the fifth month of the lunar calendar, when people celebrate the Dragon Boat Festival, it is also the time of the year that the "toxics" or "bacteria" are most active in the air. And people will be able to "cast out the toxics" and keep healthy by drinking Realgar wine.

Moon Festival/Mid-Autumn Festival

Moon Cake 月餅 yuèbing

This round-shaped cake is meant to symbolize the full moon. Wrapped inside the dough are all kinds of stuffing. Interesting patterns are imprinted on the cake.

The Winter Solstice

Rice Ball Soup 湯圓 tāngyuán

This sweet rice ball soup is very often packed with ground sesame, peanuts, or anything that you name it. People cook the rice balls in boiling water before they add sugar to the water. The globe-like rice balls are symbols of family reunification and a celebration of the peaceful and happy year that has just gone by.

Traditional Chinese Festivals

The 1st day of the 1st lunar month

| Chinese New Year | ▶ Chūn Jié | 春節 |

The 15th day of the 1st lunar month

| Lantern Festival | ▶ Yuánxiāo Jié | 元宵節 |

April 4, 5, or 6

| Tomb-Sweeping Day | ▶ Qīngmíng Jié | 清明節 |

The 8th day of the 4th lunar month

| Buddha's Birthday | ▶ Yùfó Jié | 浴佛節 |

The 5th day of the 5th lunar month		
Dragon Boat Festival ▶	Duānwǔ Jié	端午節
The 7th day of the 7th lunar month		
Chinese Valentine's Day ▶	Qīxī	七夕
The 15th day of the 7th lunar month		
Ghost Festival ▶	Zhōngyuán Jié	中元節
The 15th day of the 8th lunar month		
Moon Festival ▶	Zhōngqiū Jié	中秋節
The 15th day of the 9th lunar month		
Double Ninth Festival ▶	Chóngyáng Jié	重陽節
December 21, 22, or 23		
The Winter Solstice ▶	Dōngzhì	冬至

The Lunar Calendar

The Lunar Calendar is based on the cycle of the moon, differing therefore from the Gregorian solar calendar that is commonly used nowadays. In a lunar year, the longer months only have 30 days, while the shorter months have 29. Therefore, every 19 years sees the addition of seven intercalary months. Traditional Chinese festivals are held according to the Lunar Calendar date. However, some traditional festivals are now celebrated based on the Gregorian solar calendar. For instance, the Tomb-Sweeping Day falls on April 5, while people celebrate the Winter Solstice on the 22nd or 23rd day of December.

4 *Taking Photos*

Can I take pictures?

Wǒ kěyǐ zhàoxiàng ma?

我可以照相嗎？

Could you take a photo of me?

Kěyǐ bāng wǒ zhàoxiàng ma?

可以幫我照相嗎？

Just push the shutter.

Àn kuàimén jiù xíng le.

按快門就行了。

May I use a flashgun?

Kěyǐ yòng shǎnguāngdēng ma?

可以用閃光燈嗎？

Could I have my picture taken with you?

Wǒ kěyǐ gēn nǐ hézhào ma?

我可以跟你合照嗎？

Is there a charge for taking photographs?

Pāizhào yào bu yào shōu fèi?

拍照要不要收費？

I want to buy some camera film.

Wǒ yào mǎi dǐpiàn.

我要買底片。

My camera is broken. Can you fix it?

Wǒ de zhàoxiàngjī huài le. Nǐ kěyǐ xiūlǐ ma?

我的照相機壞了。你可以修理嗎？

I want to get my film developed.

Wǒ yào xǐ zhàopiàn.

我要洗照片。

I want to get a copy of this photo.

Wǒ yào jiāxǐ zhèi zhāng zhàopiàn.

我要加洗這張照片。

I want to have this photo enlarged.

Wǒ yào fàngdà zhèi zhāng zhàopiàn.

我要放大這張照片。

Word Bank 41 Photography equipment

battery	▶ diànchí	電池
camera	▶ zhàoxiàngjī	照相機
cap	▶ jìngtóugài	鏡頭蓋
film	▶ dǐpiàn	底片
filter	▶ lǜjìng	濾鏡
flashgun	▶ shǎnguāngdēng	閃光燈
lens	▶ jìngtóu	鏡頭
memory card	▶ cúnchǔkǎ	存儲卡
	▶ jìyìkǎ	記憶卡
shoulder strap	▶ bēidài	背帶
tripod	▶ sānjiǎojià	三腳架

5 *Souvenirs*

I want to buy some souvenirs.

Wǒ xiǎng mǎi jìniànpǐn.

我想買紀念品。

Where can I find a souvenir shop?

Nǎr yǒu jìniànpǐn shāngdiàn?

哪兒有紀念品商店？

Is this a replica?

Zhè shì fùzhìpǐn ma?

這是複製品嗎？

Are there any special things produced in this area?

Běndì yǒu shénme tèchǎn?

本地有什麼特產？

Do you have any unique souvenirs?

Yǒu méiyǒu tèbié de jìniànpǐn?

有沒有特別的紀念品？

Does it come with a warranty booklet?

Yǒu méiyǒu bǎodān?

有沒有保單？

Are there any other colors?

Yǒu méiyǒu biéde yánsè?

有沒有別的顏色？

Could I have a look?

Wǒ kěyǐ kànkan ma?
我可以看看嗎？

Is this handmade?

Zhè shì shǒugōng zuò de ma?
這是手工做的嗎？

Please wrap it up for me.

Qǐng bāng wǒ bāozhuāng.
請幫我包裝。

Can you send it abroad?

Kěyǐ bāng wǒ jì dào guówài ma?
可以幫我寄到國外嗎？

Word Bank 42 Typical souvenirs

antique	▶ gǔdǒng	古董
batik	▶ làrǎn	蠟染
bracelet	▶ shǒuzhuó	手鐲
bronzeware	▶ qīngtóngqì	青銅器
calligraphy	▶ shūfǎ	書法
carpet	▶ dìtǎn	地毯
cheongsam	▶ qípáo	旗袍
earthenware	▶ táoqì	陶器
embroidery	▶ cìxiù	刺繡

engraving seal	▶ zhuànkè	篆刻
fan	▶ shànzi	扇子
handicrafts	▶ shǒugōngyìpǐn	手工藝品
jade	▶ yùqì	玉器
kite	▶ fēngzheng	風箏
lacquerware	▶ qīqì	漆器
landscape painting	▶ shānshuǐhuà	山水畫
lantern	▶ dēnglong	燈籠
papercut	▶ jiǎnzhǐ	剪紙
porcelain	▶ cíqì	瓷器
scenic postcard	▶ fēngjǐng míngxìnpiàn	風景明信片
sculpture	▶ diāokèpǐn	雕刻品
silk	▶ sīchóu	絲綢
Tang Dynasty costume	▶ tángzhuāng	唐裝
tea	▶ cháyè	茶葉
teapot	▶ cháhú	茶壺
vase	▶ huāpíng	花瓶
woodcarving	▶ mùdiāo	木雕

Parts of the Chinese Pantheon

Jade Emperor 玉皇大帝 Yùhuáng Dàdì
Just like Zeus in Greek mythology, the Jade Emperor rules over the gods and deities in Chinese mythology.

Guan Yin / Bodhisattva 觀世音菩薩 Guānshìyīn Púsà
Dressed in white and holding a bottle made of jade, this God of Mercy always brings peace and happiness to the people.

Tudi Gong / Lord of the Land 土地公 Tǔdìgōng
Ruling from their wayside shrines, these deities are just like the administrators of small towns. Wherever you go, you will find them doing their jobs from their shrines.

Matzu / Goddess of Heaven 媽祖 Māzǔ
Viewed as the protector of fishermen and sailors, Matzu is worshipped in the coastal provinces of southern China.

The Goddess of Fertility 註生娘娘
Zhùshēng Niángniang

Women who pray to this Goddess of Fertility always have their dream come true. She is also the guardian of kids.

Literature Deity 文昌帝君 Wénchāng Dìjūn

This god of literature helps students pass exams and get admitted into schools.

Kuan Ti / God of Warrior 關聖帝君
Guānshèng Dìjūn

Kuan Ti was originally a brave and just general depicted in a famous novel. Later on, he was believed to protect businessmen, helping them move forward in the business world and prosper.

Gate Gods 門神 Ménshén

You will see them painted in armor on the front doors of temples. Generals from the Tang Dynasty, they never retire, and are now guarding the temple.

Sakyamuni Buddha 釋迦牟尼佛 Shìjiāmóuní Fó

The founder of Buddhism.

Maitreya Buddha 彌勒佛 Mílè Fó

This ever-smiling deity has a big round belly. He is always there to help people solve all kinds of problems and help them get out of their bad luck.

Searching for Oracles

When bothered by all kinds of problems, many Chinese people go to a temple to seek the advice of oracles. They will first draw lots for divination, and then throw two crescent-shaped woodblocks on the floor. This is called "zhì-jiǎo." If, for three consecutive times, one of the woodblocks turns upward, and the other downward, then you know the god is willing to respond and the answer is right there. All you have to do is go find the oracle according to the number on your lot.

Shopping

1 *About Money*

Note 10

Wanna change money?
Look for this sign,
and it'll be done!

匯 兌
huìduì

Where can I change foreign currencies?

Qǐngwèn nǎr kěyǐ huàn wàibì?
請問哪兒可以換外幣？

May I cash my traveler's checks here?

Zhèr kěyǐ huàn lǚxíng zhīpiào ma?
這兒可以換旅行支票嗎？

Where can I withdraw money on my credit card?

Nǎr kěyǐ yòng xìnyòngkǎ tíkuǎn?
哪兒可以用信用卡提款？

Where is the ATM machine?

Tíkuǎnjī zài nǎr?
提款機在哪兒？

I want to change money.

Wǒ yào jiéhuì.
我要結匯。

I want to change this into Hong Kong dollars.

Wǒ xiǎng huàn gǎngbì.

我想換港幣。

Do you accept traveler's checks?

Kěyǐ yòng lǚxíng zhīpiào ma?

可以用旅行支票嗎？

What's the maximum amount for changing money?

Zuìduō kěyǐ jié duōshao qián?

最多可以結多少錢？

Please fill out this form.

Qǐng tián biǎo.

請填表。

Word Bank 43 Some currencies

Australian dollar	àoyuán	澳元
British pound	yīngbàng	英鎊
Euro	ōuyuán	歐元
Hong Kong dollar	gǎngbì	港幣
New Taiwan dollar	xīntáibì	新台幣
New Zealand dollar	xīnxīlányuán	新西蘭元
	niǔxīlánbì	紐西蘭幣
Renminbi	rénmínbì	人民幣
U.S. dollar	měijīn	美金

Please sign here.

Qǐng qiānmíng.
請簽名。

May I have a look at your passport?

Qǐng ràng wǒ kànkan nín de hùzhào.
請讓我看看您的護照。

The exchange rate for today is 1 U.S. dollar to 7.8 Renminbi.

Jīntiān de huìlǜ shì yì měijīn duì qī diǎn bā rénmínbì.
今天的匯率是1美金兌7.8人民幣。

I'd like to change 500 U.S. dollars.

Wǒ yào jié wǔbǎi kuài měijīn.
我要結500塊美金。

That equals 3,900 Renminbi.

Děngyú sānqiān jiǔbǎi yuán rénmínbì.
等於3,900元人民幣。

Please give me some 100-dollar bills.

Qǐng gěi wǒ yìxiē yìbǎi kuài qián de chāopiào.
請給我一些100塊錢的鈔票。

I need some small change.

Wǒ xūyào língqián.
我需要零錢。

I'd like thirty-nine 100-dollar bills.

Wǒ yào sānshíjiǔ zhāng yìbǎi kuài.

我要 39 張 100 塊。

The amount is not right.

Shùmù bú duì.

數目不對。

Please check again.

Qǐng zài suàn yí cì.

請再算一次。

There is a handling fee of 39 dollars.

Shǒuxùfèi sānshíjiǔ kuài qián.

手續費 39 塊錢。

Please deduct the handling fee from the sum.

Shǒuxùfèi qǐng nèikòu.

手續費請內扣。

I'll pay the handling fee in cash.

Shǒuxùfèi lìngwài fù.

手續費另外付。

Can I have a receipt?

Yǒu méiyǒu shōujù?

有沒有收據？

2 *Making a Purchase*

Where is the menswear department, please?

Qǐngwèn nánzhuāngbù zài nǎr?
請問男裝部在哪兒？

The menswear department is on the eighth floor.

Nánzhuāngbù zài bā lóu.
男裝部在八樓。

On which floor is the food court?

Měishíjiē zài jǐ lóu?
美食街在幾樓？

(In an elevator) Tenth floor, please.

Máfan dào shí lóu.
麻煩到十樓。

May I help you?

Xūyào shénme ma?
需要什麼嗎？

I am just looking.

Wǒ zhǐshì suíbiàn kànkan.
我只是隨便看看。

Do you have perfume?

Yǒu méiyǒu xiāngshuǐ?
有沒有香水？

Word Bank 44 In a department store

bakery	▶ miànbāodiàn	麵包店
bedding	▶ qǐnjùbù	寢具部
cashier	▶ fùkuǎnchù	付款處
	▶ shōuyíntái	收銀台
coffee shop	▶ kāfēiguǎn	咖啡館
	▶ kāfēizuò	咖啡座
elevator	▶ diàntī	電梯
entrance	▶ rùkǒu	入口
escalator	▶ shǒufú diàntī	手扶電梯
	▶ diànfútī	電扶梯
exit	▶ chūkǒu	出口
food court	▶ měishíjiē	美食街
home furnishings	▶ jiājùbù	家具部
	▶ jiāshìbù	家飾部
information	▶ wènxùnchù	問訊處
	▶ xúnwènchù	詢問處
locker	▶ cúnbāoguì	存包櫃
	▶ jìwùxiāng	寄物箱
lost-and-found	▶ shīwù zhāolǐngchù	失物招領處
playground	▶ yóulèchǎng	遊樂場
restroom	▶ wèishēngjiān	衛生間
	▶ xǐshǒujiān	洗手間

stairs	▶ lóutī	樓梯
tableware	▶ cānjùbù	餐具部
toy shops	▶ wánjùbù	玩具部

Do you have this brand?

Yǒu zhèige pǐnpái ma?
有這個品牌嗎？

I'd like to have a look at the catalog.

Wǒ xiǎng kànkan mùlù.
我想看看目錄。

Can I have a look at this?

Kěyǐ kànkan zhèige ma?
可以看看這個嗎？

What is this made of?

Zhè shì shénme cáiliào?
這是什麼材料？

It's made of wood.

Zhè shì mùtou zuò de.
這是木頭做的。

Does it come with an instruction booklet?

Fù shuōmíngshū ma?
附說明書嗎？

Is there a warranty booklet inside?

Yǒu bǎodān ma?
有保單嗎？

Do you offer a warranty?

Yǒu méiyǒu bǎoxiūqī?
有沒有保修期？

Word Bank 45 Materials

bamboo	zhúzi	竹子
bone china	gǔcí	骨瓷
cotton	mián	棉
denim	niúzǎibù	牛仔布
earthenware	táoqì	陶器
fabric	bùliào	布料
glass	bōli	玻璃
leather	pígé	皮革
linen	má	麻
man-made fiber	rénzào xiānwéi	人造纖維
marble	dàlǐshí	大理石
non-woven fabric	bùzhībù	不織布
porcelain	cíqì	瓷器

silk	▶ sīchóu	絲綢
suede	▶ jǐpí	鹿皮
synthetic fiber	▶ héchéng xiānwéi	合成纖維
wood	▶ mùtou	木頭
wool	▶ máoliào	毛料

Please wrap it.

Qǐng bāng wǒ bāo qilai.
請幫我包起來。

Please wrap these separately.

Qǐng fēnkāi bāozhuāng.
請分開包裝。

Please wrap these together.

Qǐng bāo zài yìqǐ.
請包在一起。

Please gift-wrap it.

Qǐng bāozhuāng chéng lǐwù.
請包裝成禮物。

Please take off the price tag.

Qǐng bǎ biāoqiān sī xialai.
請把標籤撕下來。

Please put them in boxes.

Qǐng yòng hézi zhuāng.
請用盒子裝。

Please put them in bags.

Qǐng yòng dàizi zhuāng qilai.
請用袋子裝起來。

Can you send it to this address?

Néng bu néng bāng wǒ sòngdào zhège
dìzhǐ?
能不能幫我送到這個地址？

Could you deliver this to my hotel?

Kěyǐ bāng wǒ sòngdào fàndiàn ma?
可以幫我送到飯店嗎？

Could you send it to the States?

Kěyǐ bāng wǒ jìdào Měiguó ma?
可以幫我寄到美國嗎？ see p.183

How long will it cost to send by air?

Kōngyùn yào duōjiǔ?
空運要多久？

How long does it take to get there by sea?

Hǎiyùn jǐ tiān kěyǐ dào?
海運幾天可以到？

163

How much will it cost to send by express mail?

Jì kuàidì yào duōshao qián?

寄快遞要多少錢？

Do I have to pay for the postage?

Yào fù yóuzī ma?

要付郵資嗎？

Do I have to declare?

Yào bu yào shēnbào?

要不要申報？

Please pay at the cashier.

Qǐng dào fùkuǎnchù fù qián.

請到付款處付錢。

Word Bank 46 Stores

antique shop	gǔdǒngdiàn	古董店
bookstore	shūdiàn	書店
boutique	jīngpǐndiàn	精品店
CD shop	yīnxiàngdiàn	音像店
	chàngpiànháng	唱片行
convenience store	biànlì shāngdiàn	便利商店
department store	bǎihuò gōngsī	百貨公司

electrical goods store	▶ diànqì shāngdiàn	電器商店
	▶ sān C liàngfàndiàn	3C 量販店
flea market	▶ tiàozǎo shìchǎng	跳蚤市場
hypermarket	▶ chāojí shāngchǎng	超級商場
	▶ liàngfàndiàn	量販店
jade market	▶ yùshì	玉市
jewelry shop	▶ zhūbǎodiàn	珠寶店
market	▶ shìchǎng	市場
night market	▶ yèshì	夜市
shoe shop	▶ xiédiàn	鞋店
shopping mall	▶ dàxíng gòuwù shāngchǎng	大型購物商場
	▶ gòuwù zhōngxīn	購物中心
souvenir shop	▶ jìniànpǐn shāngdiàn	紀念品商店
sports equipment store	▶ yùndòng yòngpǐndiàn	運動用品店
supermarket	▶ chāojí shìchǎng	超級市場
toy shop	▶ wánjùdiàn	玩具店

⭐ Please see p.298 for **Shopping List**.

3 Clothes & Shoes

I am looking for a sweater.

Wǒ xiǎng mǎi yí jiàn máoyī.

我想買一件毛衣。

Do you have anything made of silk?

Yǒu méiyǒu sīchóu de?

有沒有絲綢的？

Is this real leather?

Zhè shì zhēnpí de ma?

這是真皮的嗎？

Is this made of pure cotton?

Zhè shì chúnmián de ma?

這是純棉的嗎？

May I try it on?

Néng bu néng shìchuān?

能不能試穿？

Sure.

Dāngrán kěyǐ.

當然可以。

Sorry, you can't try it on.

Duìbuqǐ, bù néng shìchuān.

對不起，不能試穿。

Where is the fitting room?

Gēngyīshì zài nǎr?
更衣室在哪兒？

Do you have this in red?

Yǒu méiyǒu hóng de?
有沒有紅的？

Word Bank 47 Colors

azure	▶ tiānlán	天藍
beige	▶ mǐsè	米色
	▶ mǐbái	米白
black	▶ hēi	黑
blue	▶ lán	藍
brown	▶ hè	褐
gray	▶ huī	灰
green	▶ lǜ	綠
khaki	▶ kǎqí	卡其
mauve	▶ fěnzǐ	粉紫
olive	▶ gǎnlǎnlǜ	橄欖綠
orange	▶ jú	橘
pink	▶ fěnhóng	粉紅
purple	▶ zǐ	紫
red	▶ hóng	紅

| white | ▶ bái | 白 |
| yellow | ▶ huáng | 黃 |

Do you have any other patterns?

Yǒu méiyǒu biéde túʻàn?

有沒有別的圖案？

Do you have something in bold stripes?

Yǒu méiyǒu cū tiáowén de?

有沒有粗條紋的？

Word Bank 48 Patterns

bold stripe	▶ cū tiáowén	粗條紋
dot	▶ yuándiǎn	圓點
gingham	▶ fānggé	方格
pinstripe	▶ xì tiáowén	細條紋
plaid	▶ gézi	格子
polka dot	▶ yuándiǎn huāwén	圓點花紋
print	▶ yìnhuā	印花
solid color	▶ sùsè	素色
striped	▶ tiáowén	條紋

It's too flashy.

Tài huāshao le.
太花哨了。

It's too plain.

Tài pǔsù le.
太樸素了。

What size is this shirt?

Zhè jiàn chènshān shì shénme chǐcùn?
這件襯衫是什麼尺寸？

I don't know my size.

Wǒ bù zhīdao wǒ gāi chuān jǐ hào.
我不知道我該穿幾號。

Could you take my measurements?

Néng bu néng bāng wǒ liáng yíxià?
能不能幫我量一下？

I need a small size.

Wǒ yào xiǎohào de.
我要小號的。

It's too small.

Tài xiǎo le.
太小了。

I want a bigger one.

Wǒ yào dà yìdiǎr de.
我要大一點兒的。

It's too tight around the hips.

Túnbù tài jǐn le.
臀部太緊了。

Can you take in the waist?

Yāowéi néng bu néng gǎi yíxià?
腰圍能不能改一下？

When can I pick it up?

Shénme shíhou kěyǐ lái ná?
什麼時候可以來拿？

I will pick it up tomorrow night.

Wǒ míngtiān wǎnshang lái ná.
我明天晚上來拿。

Can you have someone deliver it to my hotel?

Kěyǐ bāng wǒ sòngdào lǚguǎn qù ma?
可以幫我送到旅館去嗎？

Word Bank 49 About size

extra large	▶ tèdàhào	特大號
large	▶ dàhào	大號
medium	▶ zhōnghào	中號
small	▶ xiǎohào	小號
long	▶ cháng	長
short	▶ duǎn	短
loose	▶ sōng	鬆
tight	▶ jǐn	緊
thick	▶ hòu	厚
thin	▶ báo	薄

4 *Bargaining*

How much is this?

Zhège duōshao qián?
這個多少錢？

Three hundred dollars.

Sānbǎi kuài qián.
三百塊錢。

How much is this per kilo?

Zhège yì gōngjīn duōshao qián?
這個一公斤多少錢？

Twenty dollars per kilo.

Yì gōngjīn èrshí kuài qián.
一公斤二十塊錢。 ▶ see p.318

I'd like to have 500 grams of this.

Wǒ yào wǔbǎi kè.
我要五百克。

Is sales tax included?

Hán bu hán yíngyèshuì?
含不含營業稅？

That's too expensive.

Tài guì le.
太貴了。

Can you give me a five-dollar discount?

Néng bu néng piányi wǔ kuài qián?

能不能便宜五塊錢？

I'll give you a 20% discount.

Wǒ gěi nín dǎ bā zhé.

我給您打八折。

Do you have anything less expensive?

Yǒu méiyǒu piányi yìdiǎr de dōngxi?

有沒有便宜一點兒的東西？

If it was a little cheaper, I'd buy it.

Piányi yìdiǎr wǒ jiù mǎi.

便宜一點兒我就買。

I'll think about it.

Wǒ zài kǎolǜ kǎolǜ.

我再考慮考慮。

Do You Know? ⓱ **About price**

1. Throughout this region, sales tax is normally included in the listed price.

2. Discounts in Chinese are expressed very differently from in English. For example, people would say "bā zhé (80%)" for 20% off. So you can extrapolate from there that "qī zhé (70%)" would be 30% off.

5 *At the Cashier*

That's 500 dollars in total.

Yígòng wǔbǎi kuài qián.
一共五百塊錢。

Are you paying by cash or credit card?

Fùxiàn háishi shuākǎ?
付現還是刷卡？

Credit card, please.

Wǒ yào shuākǎ.
我要刷卡。

Do you accept Amex?

Nǐmen shōu Yùntōngkǎ ma?
你們收運通卡嗎？

We only take MasterCard.

Wǒmen zhǐ shōu Wànshìdákǎ.
我們只收萬事達卡。

We don't take Visa.

Wǒmen bù shōu Visa kǎ.
我們不收 Visa 卡。

Please sign here.

Qǐng zài zhèr qiānmíng.
請在這兒簽名。

Sorry, we take cash only.

Duìbuqǐ, wǒmen zhǐ shōu xiànjīn.

對不起，我們只收現金。

Can I pay in U.S. dollars?

Wǒ kěyǐ fù měijīn ma?

我可以付美金嗎？

Sorry, we take Renminbi only.

Duìbuqǐ, wǒmen zhǐ shōu rénmínbì.

對不起，我們只收人民幣。

This is your invoice.

Zhè shì nín de fāpiào.

這是您的發票。

Please give me the receipt.

Qǐng gěi wǒ shōujù.

請給我收據。

I already paid.

Wǒ yǐjīng fùguo qián le.

我已經付過錢了。

You haven't given me my change yet.

Nǐ hái méi zhǎo wǒ qián.

你還沒找我錢。

Could you check it again?

Néng bu néng zài suàn yí cì?

能不能再算一次？

6 Returns & Exchanges

Can I exchange this?

Néng bu néng tuìhuàn?
能不能退換？

What is the time limit for returning goods?

Jǐ tiān yǐnèi kěyǐ tuì huò?
幾天以內可以退貨？

I bought it yesterday.

Wǒ shì zuótiān mǎi de.
我是昨天買的。

I haven't used it at all.

Wǒ hái méi yòngguo.
我還沒用過。

This was broken when I took it out of the box.

Wǒ cóng xiāngzi li ná chulai jiù huài le.
我從箱子裡拿出來就壞了。

This is not what I bought.

Zhè bú shì wǒ mǎi de dōngxi.
這不是我買的東西。

It's got a scratch.

Zhèr yǒu ge guāhén.
這兒有個刮痕。

There's a stain on it.

Zhè shàngtou zāng le.

這上頭髒了。

The zipper doesn't work well.

Lāliàn huài le.

拉鍊壞了。

A button is gone.

Diàole yì kē kòuzi.

掉了一顆鈕子。

Can I have a refund?

Kěyǐ tuì qián ma?

可以退錢嗎？

Can I exchange it for something else?

Kěyǐ huàn biéde dōngxi ma?

可以換別的東西嗎？

Could you give me a new one?

Kěyǐ gěi wǒ yí ge xīn de ma?

可以給我一個新的嗎？

I have the invoice with me.

Wǒ dàile fāpiào lái.

我帶了發票來。

Here is the receipt.

Zhè shì shōujù.

這是收據。

Do You Know? 18 Clothes & shoes size conversion table

SHOPPING

Men's Suits

China (cm)	165/ 88-90	170/ 96-98	175/ 108-110	180/ 118-122	185/ 126-130
Intl.	S	M	L	XL	XXL

Men's Shirts

China	36-37	38-39	40-42	43-44	45-47
Intl.	S	M	L	XL	XXL

Ladies' Dress

China (cm)	160-165/ 84-86	165-170/ 88-90	167-172/ 92-96	168-173/ 98-102	170-176/ 106-110
Intl.	XS	S	M	L	XL
U.S.	2	4-6	8-10	12-14	16-18
Europe	34	34-36	38-40	42	44

Men's Shoes

China	39	40	41	42	43	44	45	46
U.S.	7	7.5	8	8.5	9	9.5	10	10.5
U.K.	6	6.5	7	7.5	8	8.5	9	9.5
Europe	39	40	41	42	43	44	45	46

Ladies' Shoes

China	35	36	37	38	39	39	40	40
U.S.	5	5.5	6	6.5	7	7.5	8	8.5
U.K.	4	4.5	5	5.5	6	6.5	7	7.5
Europe	35	36	37	38	39	39	40	40

Connecting

1. Post Office
2. Telephone
3. Fax & Photocopy
4. The Internet

1 Post Office

I want to buy some airmail letters.

Wǒ yào mǎi hángkōng xìn.
我要買航空信。

I want to buy 3 five-dollar stamps.

Wǒ yào mǎi sān zhāng wǔ kuài qián de yóupiào.
我要買三張五塊錢的郵票。

I want to send a parcel.

Wǒ yào jì bāoguǒ.
我要寄包裹。

I want to post this to Shanghai.

Wǒ yào jìdào Shànghǎi.
我要寄到上海。

I'd like a carton.

Wǒ xiǎng yào yí ge zhǐxiāng.
我想要一個紙箱。

How much does it cost?

Yóufèi duōshao qián?
郵費多少錢？

Please weigh this for me.

Qǐng nǐ chēng yíxià.
請你稱一下。

It's over the weight limit.

Chāozhòng le.
超重了。

How much extra do I need to pay?

Hái yào jiā duōshao qián?
還要加多少錢？

Fifteen dollars extra.

Zài jiā shíwǔ kuài qián.
再加十五塊錢。

What's inside?

Lǐmian shì shénme?
裡面是什麼？

Some books.

Lǐmian shì shū.
裡面是書。

I want to send it by registered mail.

Wǒ yào jì guàhào.
我要寄掛號。

I want to send this by express mail.

Wǒ yào jì kuàidì.
我要寄快遞。

Will it arrive by this afternoon?

Jīntiān xiàwǔ kěyǐ dào ma?
今天下午可以到嗎？

Where should I write the address?

Dìzhǐ yào xiě zài nǎr?

地址要寫在哪兒？

Please fill out this form.

Qǐng nín tián biǎo.

請您填表。

Please write down your phone number.

Qǐng nín xiěshang diànhuà hàomǎ.

請您寫上電話號碼。

Is that all?

Zhèyàng jiù hǎo le ma?

這樣就好了嗎？

Please wrap it.

Qǐng nǐ bāo qilai.

請你包起來。

Is there a packing machine here?

Zhèr yǒu dǎbāojī ma?

這兒有打包機嗎？

Be careful, this is fragile.

Xiǎoxīn, zhè shì yìsuì wùpǐn.

小心，這是易碎物品。

This side faces upwards.

Zhè yí miàn cháo shàng.

這一面朝上。

Word Bank 50 At post office

address	▶ dìzhǐ	地址
addressee	▶ shōujiànrén	收件人
by air	▶ kōngyùn	空運
by sea	▶ hǎiyùn	海運
envelope	▶ xìnfēng	信封
express mail	▶ kuàidì	快遞
letter	▶ xìn	信
name	▶ míngzi	名字
parcel	▶ bāoguǒ	包裹
post box	▶ yóutǒng	郵筒
post office	▶ yóujú	郵局
postcard	▶ míngxìnpiàn	明信片
registered mail	▶ guàhào	掛號
rope	▶ shéngzi	繩子
scissors	▶ jiǎndāo	剪刀
sender	▶ jìjiànrén	寄件人
stamp	▶ yóupiào	郵票
tape	▶ jiāodài	膠帶
writing paper	▶ xìnzhǐ	信紙
zip code	▶ yóuzhèng biānmǎ	郵政編碼
	▶ yóudì qūhào	郵遞區號

CONNECTING

2 *Telephone*

I want to make an international phone call.

Wǒ yào dǎ guójì diànhuà.
我要打國際電話。

I want to make a call to Beijing.

Wǒ yào dǎ diànhuà dào Běijīng.
我要打電話到北京。

Can I call directly?

Shì zhíbō de ma?
是直撥的嗎？

No, an operator will put you through.

Búshì, yóu jiēxiànyuán zhuǎnjiē.
不是，由接線員轉接。

I want to make a collect call.

Wǒ xiǎng dǎ duìfāng fùfèi de diànhuà.
我想打對方付費的電話。

Where can I find a public telephone booth?

Nǎr yǒu gōngyòng diànhuà?
哪兒有公用電話？

Could I borrow your phone?

Kěyǐ jièyòng nǐ de diànhuà ma?
可以借用你的電話嗎？

How do I use this phone?

Zhèige diànhuà zěnme yòng?

這個電話怎麼用？

Do I have to insert coins?

Yào tóubì ma?

要投幣嗎？

How many coins should I insert?

Yào tóu duōshao qián?

要投多少錢？

Can I call with a phone card?

Kěyǐ shǐyòng diànhuàkǎ ma?

可以使用電話卡嗎？

I'd like to buy a 100-dollar phone card.

Wǒ yào mǎi yìbǎi kuài de diànhuàkǎ.

我要買一百塊的電話卡。

Can I make an international call with this phone?

Zhèige diànhuà kěyǐ dǎ guójì diànhuà ma?

這個電話可以打國際電話嗎？

How much is the charge?

Diànhuàfèi zěnme suàn?

電話費怎麼算？

This is a long-distance call. It will be more expensive.

Zhè shì chángtú diànhuà, bǐjiào guì.

這是長途電話，比較貴。

Two dollars per second.

Yì miǎozhōng liǎng kuài qián.

一秒鐘兩塊錢。

What number should I dial?

Wǒ yīnggāi bō jǐ hào?

我應該撥幾號？

First dial 9, then the number.

Qǐng nín xiān bō jiǔ, zài bō diànhuà hàomǎ.

請您先撥 9，再撥電話號碼。

CONNECTING

(In a restaurant or an office) What number should I dial first if I am making a phone call?

Dǎ wàixiàn yào bō jǐ hào?

打外線要撥幾號？

What's the phone number?

Diànhuà hàomǎ shì jǐ hào?

電話號碼是幾號？

Is this your home phone number or is this the number of your office?

Zhè shì jiā li de diànhuà háishi gōngsī de diànhuà?

這是家裡的電話還是公司的電話？

What's the area code?

Qūyù hàomǎ shì jǐ hào?

區域號碼是幾號？

What's your cell phone number?

Nǐ de shǒujī shì jǐ hào?

你的手機是幾號？

What's your extension number?

Nǐ de fēnjī shì jǐ hào?

你的分機是幾號？

Is there a contact number in case of an emergency?

Yǒu méiyǒu jǐnjí liánluò diànhuà?

有沒有緊急聯絡電話？

Do you have a telephone book?

Yǒu méiyǒu diànhuàbù?

有沒有電話簿？

I can't get through.

Diànhuà dǎ bu tōng.

電話打不通。

The line is busy.

Diànhuà zhànxiàn.

電話佔線。

Is this the Chang-Qiao Company?

Shì Chángqiáo Gōngsī ma?

是長橋公司嗎？

Hello, I'd like to talk to Mr. Zhang, the manager.

Wéi, wǒ yào zhǎo Zhāng jīnglǐ.

喂，我要找張經理。

Please wait a moment.

Qǐng děng yíxià (Qǐng shāo děng).
請等一下（請稍等）。

Is Mr. Zhang, the manager, in, please?

Zhāng jīnglǐ zài ma?
張經理在嗎？

Speaking.

Wǒ jiù shì.
我就是。

He is not around.

Tā bú zài.
他不在。

Who is calling, please?

Nín shì něi wèi?
您是哪位？

My name is Peter. I am his friend.

Wǒ jiào Peter, shì tā de péngyou.
我叫 Peter，是他的朋友。

When will he be back?

Tā shénme shíhou huílai?
他什麼時候回來？

May I have your phone number, please?

Nín yào liú ge diànhuà ma?
您要留個電話嗎？

My number is 2431-9905.

Wǒ de diànhuà shì èr sì sān yāo jiǔ jiǔ líng wǔ.

我的電話是 2431-9905。 ▶ see p.16

I want to leave a message for him.

Wǒ yào liúhuà.

我要留話。

Please ask him to return my call.

Qǐng tā huí diànhuà gěi wǒ.

請他回電話給我。

Sorry, I've got the wrong number.

Duìbuqǐ, wǒ dǎcuò le.

對不起，我打錯了。

I can't hear you very clearly.

Wǒ tīng bù qīngchu.

我聽不清楚。

Could you please say that again?

Qǐng zài shuō yí biàn.

請再說一遍。

Could you speak up, please?

Qǐng dà yìdiǎr shēng shuō.

請大一點兒聲說。

Please speak a little slower.

Qǐng màn yìdiǎr shuō.

請慢一點兒說。

CONNECTING

189

In large cities, pay phones are to be found readily in most public places and literally on every corner of the street. There are two types of pay phones: one takes coins; the other needs a phone card. For budget international calls, go to larger stores and ask the shop owners, "Do you have a phone card for international calls?" "Yǒu guójì diànhuàkǎ ma?" and you will get it. But for local calls, you are usually better off with a local card. Aside from coins and phone cards, in most major cities, look for phones with a credit card sign, which means you can make a phone call by inserting your credit card.

When visiting small towns and villages, you may have to find kiosks with a sign saying "電話 (diànhuà)," or "telephone." From these kiosks, you may call literally anywhere, however, negotiating the price in advance is a must. Moreover, in these places, only cash is accepted.

If you are encountering language problems, you may of course call from your room in the hotel. An operator will put you through, but of course, good customer service costs.

3 *Fax & Photocopy*

Is it possible to send a fax here?

Zhèr kěyǐ chuánzhēn ma?

這兒可以傳真嗎？

Where can I find a fax machine?

Nǎr yǒu chuánzhēnjī?

哪兒有傳真機？

I want to fax a document.

Wǒ yào chuán yí fèn wénjiàn.

我要傳一份文件。

What is your fax number?

Nín de chuánzhēn hàomǎ shì jǐ hào?

您的傳真號碼是幾號？

My fax number is 2437-9921.

Wǒ de chuánzhēn hàomǎ shì èr sì sān qī jiǔ jiǔ èr yāo.

我的傳真號碼是 2437-9921。

Could I receive faxes here?

Zhèr kěyǐ shōu chuánzhēn ma?

這兒可以收傳真嗎？

Can I send a fax through the Internet?

Wǒ kěyǐ yòng Yīntèwǎng chuánzhēn ma?
我可以用因特網傳真嗎？

Can I make a photocopy here?

Zhèr kěyǐ fùyìn ma?
這兒可以複印嗎？

Please photocopy this document for me.

Qǐng bāng wǒ fùyìn zhèi fèn wénjiàn.
請幫我複印這份文件。

How do I operate this?

Zěnme cāozuò?
怎麼操作？

Press this button.

Àn zhèige jiàn.
按這個鍵。

You need to insert coins.

Nín yào tóubì.
您要投幣。

You need to buy a card.

Nín yào mǎi fùyìnkǎ.
您要買複印卡。

4 *The Internet*

Do you have an email account?

Nǐ yǒu méiyǒu diànzǐ yóuxiāng?
你有沒有電子郵箱？

Do you have your own Web site?

Nǐ yǒu méiyǒu zìjǐ de wǎngzhàn?
你有沒有自己的網站？

Please tell me your Web site address.

Qǐng gàosu wǒ nǐ de wǎngzhǐ.
請告訴我你的網址。

Are there any Internet café near here?

Zhè fùjìn yǒu méiyǒu wǎngbā?
這附近有沒有網吧？

Is Internet access available here?

Zhèr kěyǐ shàngwǎng ma?
這兒可以上網嗎？

Can this computer display German?

Néng bu néng xiǎnshì Déwén?
能不能顯示德文？

Can this computer display French?

Néng bu néng xiǎnshì Fǎwén?
能不能顯示法文？

How much do you charge?

Fèiyong zěnme suàn?
費用怎麼算？

Five dollars per hour.

Yì xiǎoshí wǔ kuài qián.
一小時五塊錢。

Word Bank 51 About computer

broadband	▶ kuānpín	寬頻
CD-ROM	▶ guāngpán	光盤
	▶ guāngdié	光碟
computer	▶ diànnǎo	電腦
disk	▶ ruǎnpán	軟盤
	▶ cídiépiàn	磁碟片
keyboard	▶ jiànpán	鍵盤
mainframe	▶ zhǔjī	主機
monitor	▶ yíngguāngpíng	螢光屏
	▶ yíngmù	螢幕
mouse	▶ shǔbiāo	鼠標
	▶ huáshǔ	滑鼠
notebook computer	▶ bǐjìběn diànnǎo	筆記本電腦
	▶ bǐjìxíng diànnǎo	筆記型電腦
printer	▶ dǎyìnjī	打印機
	▶ yìnbiǎojī	印表機

scanner	▶ sǎomiáoyí ▶ sǎomiáoqì	掃描儀 掃描器
USB flash drive	▶ suíshēndié	隨身碟
wireless network	▶ wúxiàn shàngwǎng ▶ wúxiàn wǎnglù	無線上網 無線網路

CONNECTING

Notes

Making Chinese Friends

1 *Self Introduction*

May I have your name, please? (formal)

Nín guìxìng dàmíng?

您貴姓大名？

What's your name? (informal)

Nǐ jiào shénme míngzi?

你叫什麼名字？

Note ⑪

In inquiring a stranger's name, the honorific term "Nín guìxìng dàmíng?" is used when the party addressed appears to be a social superior. But if you are sure it's a social equal that you are speaking to, you would say "Nǐ jiào shénme míngzi?" instead.

My family name is Wang, and my given name is Daming.

Wǒ xìng Wáng, jiào Dàmíng.

我姓王，叫大明。

My name is Wang Daming.

Wǒ jiào Wáng Dàmíng.

我叫王大明。

Nice to meet you, Mr. Wang. (informal)

Hěn gāoxìng rènshi nǐ, Wáng xiānsheng.
很高興認識你，王先生。

My great honor to meet you, Miss Lin. (formal)

Xìnghuì, xìnghuì, Lín xiǎojie.
幸會，幸會，林小姐。

May I introduce myself?

Wǒ jièshào yíxià zìjǐ, kěyǐ ma?
我介紹一下自己，可以嗎？

What do you do?

Nǐ shì zuò shénme de?
你是做什麼的？

I am a student.

Wǒ shì xuésheng.
我是學生。

Where are you from?

Nǐ shì cóng nǎr lái de?
你是從哪兒來的？

I am from the U.S.

Wǒ shì cóng Měiguó lái de.
我是從美國來的。

Are you married?

Nǐ jiéhūn le ma?
你結婚了嗎？

I am married.

Wǒ jiéhūn le.
我結婚了。

I am single.

Wǒ dānshēn.
我單身。

Do you have children?

Nǐ yǒu méiyǒu háizi?
你有沒有孩子？

I have one son.

Wǒ yǒu yí ge érzi.
我有一個兒子。

Are you here alone?

Nǐ yí ge rén lái ma?
你一個人來嗎？

I am here alone.

Wǒ yí ge rén lái.
我一個人來。

I am here with my fiancée.

Wǒ gēn wǒ wèihūnqī yíkuàr lái.
我跟我未婚妻一塊兒來。

Word Bank 52 Occupations & job titles

accountant	kuàijìshī	會計師
businessman	shāngrén	商人
consultant	gùwèn	顧問
designer	shèjìshī	設計師
doctor	yīshēng	醫生
engineer	gōngchéngshī	工程師
government officer	gōngwùyuán	公務員
housewife	jiātíng fùnǚ jiātíng zhǔfù	家庭婦女 家庭主婦
lawyer	lǜshī	律師
nurse	hùshi	護士
researcher	yánjiūyuán	研究員
salesperson	yèwùyuán	業務員
sportsman	yùndòngyuán	運動員
teacher	lǎoshī	老師

MAKING CHINESE FRIENDS

I don't have a girlfriend.

Wǒ méiyǒu nǚpéngyou.
我沒有女朋友。

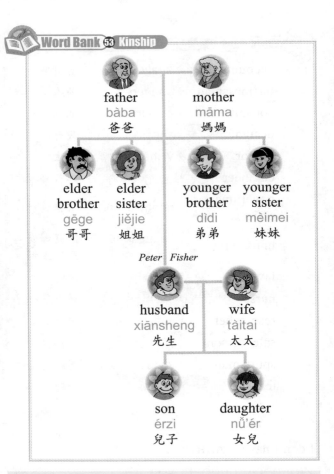

father
bàba
爸爸

mother
māma
媽媽

elder brother
gēge
哥哥

elder sister
jiějie
姐姐

younger brother
dìdi
弟弟

younger sister
mèimei
妹妹

Peter Fisher

husband
xiānsheng
先生

wife
tàitai
太太

son
érzi
兒子

daughter
nǚ'ér
女兒

MAKING CHINESE FRIENDS

This is my boyfriend.

Zhè shì wǒ nánpéngyou.

這是我男朋友。

What are you here for?

Nǐ lái zhèr zuò shénme?
你來這兒做什麼？

I am here on business.

Wǒ lái chūchāi.
我來出差。

I am here on vacation.

Wǒ lái lǚxíng.
我來旅行。

I go to school here.

Wǒ lái niànshū.
我來念書。

I am here to visit my friends.

Wǒ lái kàn péngyou.
我來看朋友。

Do You Know? 20 Hospitality

Chinese people are very kind to foreigners, sometimes with excessive passion. Sometimes they will ask you something very personal, like your marital status. Don't feel offended. This is just how they show their hospitality.

203

2 Language Difficulties

Sorry, I don't understand.

Duìbuqǐ, wǒ tīng bu dǒng.

對不起，我聽不懂。

I beg your pardon.

Qǐng zài shuō yí cì.

請再說一次。

Could you speak more slowly?

Qǐng màn yìdiǎr shuō.

請慢一點兒說。

Louder, please.

Qǐng dà yìdiǎr shēng shuō.

請大一點兒聲說。

Could you speak in English?

Máfan nǐ shuō Yīngwén.

麻煩你說英文。

Now I see.

Wǒ dǒng le.

我懂了。

I do not speak Chinese.

Wǒ bú huì shuō Zhōngwén.

我不會說中文。

I speak a little Chinese.

Wǒ huì shuō yìdiǎr Zhōngwén.
我會說一點兒中文。

Do you speak English?

Nǐ huì shuō Yīngwén ma?
你會說英文嗎？

Can I speak English?

Wǒ kěyǐ shuō Yīngwén ma?
我可以說英文嗎？

Do any of you speak English?

Nǐmen yǒu méiyǒu rén huì shuō Yīngwén?
你們有沒有人會說英文？

What are you saying?

Nǐ de yìsi shì shénme?
你的意思是什麼？

How do you write the character?

Zhège zì zěnme xiě?
這個字怎麼寫？

Could you write it down for me?

Qǐng bāng wǒ xiě xialai.
請幫我寫下來。

How do you say "ticket" in Chinese?

"Ticket" Zhōngwén zěnme shuō?
「Ticket」中文怎麼說？

3 Small Talk

Excuse me.

Bù hǎo yìsi.
不好意思。

Could I ask you something?

Qǐngjiào yíxià.
請教一下。

Yes. What is it?

Qǐng shuō.
請說。

Just a moment, please.

Qǐng děng yíxià.
請等一下。

Sorry, I'm not available now.

Duìbuqǐ, wǒ méi kòng.
對不起，我沒空。

I've got to go.

Wǒ děi zǒu le.
我得走了。

Leave me alone.

Bié fán wǒ.
別煩我。

Get lost.

Zǒukai.

走開。

How long have you been here?

Nǐ láile duōjiǔ le?

你來了多久了？

I have been here for 4 days.

Wǒ láile sì tiān le.

我來了四天了。

How long are you staying?

Nǐ dǎsuàn dāi duōjiǔ?

你打算待多久？

A couple of days.

Jǐ tiān.

幾天。

A couple of weeks.

Jǐ ge xīngqī.

幾個星期。

A couple of months.

Jǐ ge yuè.

幾個月。

I am leaving tomorrow.

Wǒ míngtiān zǒu.

我明天走。

Where are you going to?

Nǐ dǎsuàn qù nǎr?
你打算去哪兒？

I am leaving for Hong Kong.

Wǒ yào qù Xiānggǎng.
我要去香港。

I am going to a show.

Wǒ yào qù kàn biǎoyǎn.
我要去看表演。

Have you ever been to the U.S.?

Nǐ qùguo Měiguó ma?
你去過美國嗎？

How do you like it there?

Nǐ juéde nàr zěnmeyàng?
你覺得那兒怎麼樣？

This is a nice place.

Zhè shì ge hǎo dìfang.
這是個好地方。

I like it very much.

Wǒ hěn xǐhuan.
我很喜歡。

I find it all right.

Hái hǎo.
還好。

I don't like it.

Wǒ bù xǐhuan.

我不喜歡。

Do you like your job?

Nǐ xǐhuan nǐ de gōngzuò ma?

你喜歡你的工作嗎？

Where are you staying?

Nǐ zhù nǎr?

你住哪兒？

I am staying in a hotel.

Wǒ zhù lǚguǎn.

我住旅館。

I am staying at my friend's place.

Wǒ zhù péngyou jiā.

我住朋友家。

I am living at my relative's house.

Wǒ zhù qīnqi jiā.

我住親戚家。

What are your hobbies?

Nǐ yǒu shénme shìhào?

你有什麼嗜好？

I like playing tennis.

Wǒ xǐhuan dǎ wǎngqiú.

我喜歡打網球。

Do you travel a lot?

Nǐ cháng lǚxíng ma?
你常旅行嗎？

Yes, I travel quite a lot.

Shì a, wǒ cháng lǚxíng.
是啊，我常旅行。

No, I don't really travel a lot.

Wǒ bù cháng lǚxíng.
我不常旅行。

What a wonderful day!

Jīntiān tiānqì zhēn hǎo!
今天天氣真好！

It's hot today.

Jīntiān hǎo rè a!
今天好熱啊！

I like sunny days.

Wǒ xǐhuan qíngtiān.
我喜歡晴天。

I don't like rainy days.

Wǒ bù xǐhuan yǔtiān.
我不喜歡雨天。

Does it rain a lot at this time?

Zuìjìn cháng xiàyǔ ma?
最近常下雨嗎？

Does it snow here?

Zhèli huì xiàxuě ma?
這裡會下雪嗎？

 **Word Bank** 54 **Hobbies**

bungee jumping	▶ bèngjítiào	蹦極跳
	▶ gāokōng tántiào	高空彈跳
cycling	▶ qí zìxíngchē	騎自行車
dancing	▶ tiàowǔ	跳舞
gliding	▶ wán huáxiángjī	玩滑翔機
	▶ wán huáxiángyì	玩滑翔翼
horse riding	▶ qímǎ	騎馬
listening to music	▶ tīng yīnyuè	聽音樂
mountain climbing	▶ páshān	爬山
painting	▶ huàhuàr	畫畫兒

MAKING CHINESE FRIENDS

playing basketball	▶ dǎ lánqiú	打籃球
playing chess	▶ xiàqí	下棋
playing football	▶ tī zúqiú	踢足球
playing golf	▶ dǎ gāo'ěrfūqiú	打高爾夫球
playing piano	▶ tán gāngqín	彈鋼琴
playing violin	▶ lā xiǎotíqín	拉小提琴
practicing Tai Chi	▶ dǎ tàijíquán	打太極拳
practicing yoga	▶ liàn yújiā	練瑜伽
reading	▶ kànshū	看書
rock climbing	▶ yánshí pāndēng ▶ pānyán	岩石攀登 攀岩
sailing	▶ jià fānchuán	駕帆船
seeing movies	▶ kàn diànyǐng	看電影
singing	▶ chànggē	唱歌
skating	▶ huábīng ▶ liūbīng	滑冰 溜冰
skiing	▶ huáxuě	滑雪

skydiving	▶ tiàosǎn	跳傘
snowboarding	▶ wán huáxuěbǎn	玩滑雪板
traveling	▶ lǚxíng	旅行
watching TV	▶ kàn diànshì	看電視
writing	▶ xiězuò	寫作

Word Bank 55 Weather conditions

cold	▶ lěng	冷
cool	▶ liángkuai	涼快
dry	▶ gānzào	乾燥
humid	▶ cháoshī	潮濕
warm	▶ nuǎnhuo	暖和

4 Invitations & Making Appointments

Are you free tonight?

Nǐ jīntiān wǎnshang yǒu kòng ma?
你今天晚上有空嗎？

Would you like to have dinner with me?

Xiǎng bu xiǎng yíkuàr chī wǎnfàn?
想不想一塊兒吃晚飯？

Feeling like having a drink?

Xiǎng bu xiǎng hē yì bēi?
想不想喝一杯？

It's my treat today.

Jīntiān wǒ qǐngkè.
今天我請客。

Good idea.

Hǎo zhǔyi.
好主意。

Of course.

Dāngrán hǎo.
當然好。

My pleasure.

Wǒ de róngxìng.
我的榮幸。

Yes, but only after 9:00.

Hǎo a, kěshì wǒ jiǔ diǎn yǐhòu cái yǒu kòng.

好啊，可是我九點以後才有空。

No, thank you.

Bù le, xièxie nǐ.

不了，謝謝你。

I don't feel like drinking.

Wǒ bú tài xiǎng hē jiǔ.

我不太想喝酒。

I already have a date.

Wǒ yǐjīng yǒu yuē le.

我已經有約了。

I'd like to go, but I don't have time.

Wǒ hěn xiǎng qù, kěxī méi kòng.

我很想去，可惜沒空。

What are we going to do?

Wǒmen yào zuò shénme ne?

我們要做什麼呢？

How about going to a movie?

Kàn diànyǐng zěnmeyàng?

看電影怎麼樣？

I'd like to sit at the bar.

Wǒ xiǎng qù jiǔbā.

我想去酒吧。

Let's go dancing.

Wǒmen qù tiàowǔ ba.
我們去跳舞吧。

When shall we meet?

Wǒmen jǐ diǎn pèngmiàn?
我們幾點碰面？

Where shall we meet?

Wǒmen zài nǎr pèngmiàn?
我們在哪兒碰面？

I will see you in the lobby.

Wǒmen dàtīng jiàn.
我們大廳見。

I will see you at 7:30.

Wǒmen qī diǎn bàn jiàn.
我們七點半見。 see p.34

I already paid.

Wǒ yǐjīng fùguo qián le.
我已經付過錢了。

Let's meet in the bar, okay?

Wǒmen zài jiǔbā pèngmiàn, hǎo ma?
我們在酒吧碰面，好嗎？

I will call you at 7:00.

Wǒ qī diǎn dǎ diànhuà gěi nǐ.
我七點打電話給你。

5 *Visiting a Friend's House*

Is there anyone home?

Yǒu rén zài jiā ma?

有人在家嗎？

Is Wang Daming home?

Qǐngwèn Wáng Dàmíng zài jiā ma?

請問王大明在家嗎？

I have an appointment with Mr. Wang.

Wǒ gēn Wáng xiānsheng yǒu yuē.

我跟王先生有約。

Who's there?

Nǐ shì nǎ wèi?

你是哪位？

I am Peter Fisher from the States.

Wǒ shì Měiguó lái de, wǒ jiào Peter Fisher.

我是美國來的，我叫 Peter Fisher。

Welcome.

Huānyíng!

歡迎！

Please come in.

Qǐng jìn.

請進。

It's been a long time.

Hǎo jiǔ bú jiàn.
好久不見。

How nice of you to come.

Zhēn gāoxìng nǐ lái le.
真高興你來了。

Nice to have you back.

Zhēn gāoxìng nǐ huílai le.
真高興你回來了。

This is for you.

Zhè shì wǒ yìdiǎr xīnyì.
這是我一點兒心意。

How have you been doing?

Nǐ zuìjìn hǎo ma?
你最近好嗎？

How's your family?

Jiārén dōu hǎo ma?
家人都好嗎？

Everyone is fine.

Dàjiā dōu hěn hǎo.
大家都很好。

It's going pretty well.

Yíqiè dōu hěn shùnlì.
一切都很順利。

Same as usual.

Lǎo yàngzi.

老樣子。

You haven't changed at all.

Nǐ yìdiǎr dōu méi biàn.

你一點兒都沒變。

You look great!

Nǐ de qìsè hěn búcuò!

你的氣色很不錯！

Take your seat, please.

Qǐng zuò.

請坐。

Make yourself at home.

Jiù dāng zài zìjǐ jiā li yíyàng.

就當在自己家裡一樣。

Your house looks lovely.

Nǐ jiā zhēn piàoliang.

你家真漂亮。

Feel like drinking something?

Xiǎng hē diǎr shénme ma?

想喝點兒什麼嗎？

Don't mind me.

Búbì zhāohu wǒ.

不必招呼我。

May I use your bathroom?

Jiè ge wèishēngjiān, hǎo ma?
借個衛生間，好嗎？

Can I use your telephone?

Jiè ge diànhuà, hǎo ma?
借個電話，好嗎？

This is especially for you.

Zhè shì tèbié wèi nǐ zhǔnbèi de.
這是特別為你準備的。

You shouldn't have.

Nǐ tài kèqi le.
你太客氣了。

Do You Know? ㉑ Congratulations

If you are visiting your Chinese friends during the Chinese New Year or when they are holding significant events, such as a wedding, the following phrases will make you sound like an insider. But first, make sure you have "gōngxǐ," or congratulations, in your repertoire. This will help you move around easily.

Word Bank 56 Wishing you....

Happy Birthday	▶ shēngrì-kuàilè	生日快樂
Happy New Year	▶ xīnnián-kuàilè	新年快樂
Happiness (in married life)	▶ xīnhūn-yúkuài	新婚愉快
Have a nice trip	▶ yílù-shùnfēng	一路順風
Successful and Prosperous (in your career)	▶ shìyè-chénggōng	事業成功

6 Having Dinner with a Friend

What is this?

Zhè shì shénme?

這是什麼？

This is cabbage with dried shrimps.

Zhè shì shàngtāng-báicài.

這是上湯白菜。

Delicious!

Zhēn hǎochī!

真好吃！

Tastes good.

Wèidào búcuò.

味道不錯。

Make yourself at home. Help yourself.

Bié kèqi, zìjǐ lái.

別客氣，自己來。

I don't eat meat.

Wǒ bù chī ròu.

我不吃肉。

I don't drink.

Wǒ bù hē jiǔ.

我不喝酒。

Please help me with the dish.

Qǐng bāng wǒ jiā cài.

請幫我夾菜。

Please help me with the soup.

Qǐng bāng wǒ yǎo tāng.

請幫我舀湯。

Would you like to have some more wine?

Yào bu yào zài lái diǎr jiǔ?

要不要再來點兒酒？

(To offer a toast to someone) To you.

Wǒ jìng nǐ.

我敬你。

Cheers. / Bottoms up.

Gānbēi.

乾杯。

I have had enough.

Wǒ chībǎo le.

我吃飽了。

I am really full.

Wǒ zhēnde chī bu xià le.

我真的吃不下了。

(To everyone) Enjoy your meal.

Dàjiā màn yòng.

大家慢用。

Do You Know? 22 **Chinese dining etiquette**

1. The Chinese people seldom pass dishes. Instead, they help each other serving dishes.

2. Treating their guests with excessive food is one way that Chinese people express their hospitality. Therefore, despite the guests' repeated pleas, saying they really have had enough, the hosts will keep serving food. So, if you are really full, you will have to say it loud and firm, and "Wǒ zhēnde chī bu xià le," which means "I really can't eat any more" is the phrase that you need exactly at this point of time.

3. Another way that Chinese people express their hospitality is to offer their guests cigarettes or to drink a toast from time to time. You might find it troublesome when the host insists that you "Bottoms up," that is to drink up. Don't feel shy about saying "Nǐ gānbēi, wǒ suíyì." which might not have an equivalent in your language, but means literally, "while you drink up, I will just drink as much as I feel comfortable with."

4. The Chinese people do not pray before they start a meal. Normally it's the elders of the family that signal when to start.

7 *Farewell*

Nice meeting you.

Hěn gāoxìng rènshi nǐ.
很高興認識你。

Nice seeing you.

Kàndào nǐ zhēn gāoxìng.
看到你真高興。

It's getting late.

Shíhou bù zǎo le.
時候不早了。

I've got to go.

Wǒ gāi zǒu le.
我該走了。

Thank you so much.

Zhēnshì tài xièxie nǐ le.
真是太謝謝你了。

It was a lot of fun.

Wǒ wán de hěn kāixīn.
我玩得很開心。

Let's get together again sometime.

Yǒu kòng zài zhǎo shíjiān jùju.
有空再找時間聚聚。

Could you take me home?

Nǐ kěyǐ sòng wǒ huíjiā ma?

你可以送我回家嗎？

I will call you.

Wǒ huì dǎ diànhuà gěi nǐ.

我會打電話給你。

Please give me your email address.

Qǐng gěi wǒ nǐ de diànzǐ yóuxiāng.

請給我你的電子郵箱。

I will write you.

Wǒ huì xiěxìn gěi nǐ.

我會寫信給你。

I'll miss you.

Wǒ huì xiǎngniàn nǐ.

我會想念你。

Please give my regards to your family.

Qǐng dài wǒ xiàng nǐ de jiārén wènhǎo.

請代我向你的家人問好。

When will you be back?

Nǐ shénme shíhou zài lái?

你什麼時候再來？

You must come back again.

Nǐ yídìng yào zài lái.

你一定要再來。

I will be waiting for your phone call.

Wǒ huì děng nǐ de diànhuà.
我會等你的電話。

I hope to keep in touch with you.

Wǒmen yào bǎochí liánluò.
我們要保持聯絡。

I hope to see you again soon.

Xīwàng hěn kuài néng zài jiàndào nǐ.
希望很快能再見到你。

Take care.

Duō bǎozhòng.
多保重。

Goodbye.

Zàijiàn.
再見。

Have a safe trip home.

Lùshang xiǎoxīn.
路上小心。

Be careful. (while you go home)

Màn zǒu.
慢走。

Have a nice trip!

Yílù-shùnfēng!
一路順風！

Notes

Entertainment

1 *At the Box Office*

Please line up here.

Qǐng páiduì.

請排隊。

Please don't cut in line.

Qǐng bié chāduì.

請別插隊。

What's showing now?

Xiànzài shàngyǎn shénme?

現在上演什麼？

When's the next show?

Xià yì chǎng shénme shíhou kāishǐ?

下一場什麼時候開始？

Do you have matinee shows?

Yǒu wǔchǎng ma?

有午場嗎？

Are there any seats left for the evening performance?

Wǎnchǎng hái yǒu méiyǒu wèizi?

晚場還有沒有位子？

It's sold out.

Màiguāng le.

賣光了。

Your reservation is confirmed.

Nín dìng de wèizi yǐjīng quèrèn le.

您訂的位子已經確認了。

Your reservation is canceled.

Nín dìng de wèizi bèi qǔxiāo le.

您訂的位子被取消了。

When will you have seats available?

Shénme shíhou huì yǒu zuòwèi?

什麼時候會有座位？

How many tickets do you want?

Nín yào jǐ zhāng piào?

您要幾張票？

Is there a student discount?

Xuéshēngpiào yǒu méiyǒu yōuhuì?

學生票有沒有優惠？

Word Bank 57 Show times

morning performance	▸ zǎochǎng	早場
matinee	▸ wǔchǎng	午場
evening performance	▸ wǎnchǎng	晚場
late-night show	▸ wǔyèchǎng	午夜場

I'd like to have 2 adult tickets.

Wǒ yào liǎng zhāng chéngrénpiào.

我要兩張成人票。

Free admission?

Miǎnfèi rùchǎng ma?

免費入場嗎？

For which show?

Nǎ yì chǎng?

哪一場？

For the 9 o'clock show.

Jiǔ diǎn nà yì chǎng.

九點那一場。

Can I have a look at the seating chart, please?

Kěyǐ ràng wǒ kànkan zuòwèibiǎo ma?

可以讓我看看座位表嗎？

Word Bank 58 Ticket types

adult ticket	▶ chéngrénpiào	成人票
child discount	▶ értóngpiào	兒童票
discount for senior citizens	▶ lǎorénpiào	老人票
discount for students	▶ xuéshēngpiào	學生票
group discount	▶ tuántǐpiào	團體票

232

I'd like to have back row seats.

Wǒ yào hòupái zuòwèi.

我要後排座位。

I'd like to have a seat near the stage.

Wǒ yào wǔtái biān de zuòwèi.

我要舞台邊的座位。

I'd like to sit in the non-smoking area.

Wǒ yào fēixīyānqū de wèizi.

我要非吸煙區的位子。

Give me 4 seats together, please.

Qǐng bāng wǒ huà sì ge xiānglián de wèizi.

請幫我劃四個相連的位子。

Separate seats are okay.

Zuòwèi fēnkāi yě xíng.

座位分開也行。

Word Bank 59 Seat types

back row seats	▶ hòupái zuòwèi	後排座位
balcony	▶ bāoxiāng	包廂
circle	▶ èr lóu qiánpái	二樓前排
front row seats	▶ qiánpái zuòwèi	前排座位
in the center	▶ zhōngjiān zuòwèi	中間座位
standing room	▶ zhànpiàowèi	站票位

2 At a Sporting Event

I'd like to go to a baseball game.

Wǒ xiǎng qù kàn bàngqiúsài.

我想去看棒球賽。

Are there any baseball parks nearby?

Zhè fùjìn yǒu bàngqiúchǎng ma?

這附近有棒球場嗎？

What teams are playing?

Bǐsài de shì něi liǎng duì?

比賽的是哪兩隊？

The Bulls versus the Bears.

Niúduì duì Xióngduì.

牛隊對熊隊。

What time does the game begin?

Bǐsài jǐ diǎn kāishǐ?

比賽幾點開始？

When is the game estimated to end?

Yùdìng jǐ diǎn jiéshù?

預定幾點結束？

7:30.

Qī diǎn bàn.

七點半。 see p.34

234

I'd like to see the day game.

Wǒ yào kàn rìchǎng.

我要看日場。

I'd prefer a night game.

Wǒ xiǎng kàn wǎnchǎng.

我想看晚場。

I'd like a seat on the first base line.

Wǒ yào yìlěi nèiyě de piào.

我要一壘內野的票。

Where is the concession stand?

Xiǎomàibù zài nǎli?

小賣部在哪裡？

I'm a fan of the Bulls.

Wǒ shì Niúduì de qiúmí.

我是牛隊的球迷。

The Bears are beating the Bulls by 2 points.

Xióngduì lǐngxiān Niúduì liǎng fēn.

熊隊領先牛隊兩分。

The Bulls are the home team.

Niúduì shì dìzhǔduì.

牛隊是地主隊。

The visiting team is the Bears.

Kèduì shì Xióngduì.

客隊是熊隊。

What's the score?

Bǐshù shì duōshao?
比數是多少？

We won.

Wǒmen yíng le.
我們贏了。

Word Bank 60 Sports

badminton	▶ yǔmáoqiú	羽毛球
baseball	▶ bàngqiú	棒球
basketball	▶ lánqiú	籃球
billiards	▶ táiqiú ▶ zhuàngqiú	檯球 撞球
bowling	▶ bǎolíngqiú	保齡球
football	▶ měishì zúqiú	美式足球
golf	▶ gāo'ěrfūqiú	高爾夫球
jogging	▶ mànpǎo	慢跑
rollerblading	▶ zhípáilún	直排輪
rugby	▶ gǎnlǎnqiú	橄欖球
soccer	▶ yīngshì zúqiú	英式足球
table tennis	▶ pīngpāngqiú	乒乓球
tennis	▶ wǎngqiú	網球

They lost.

Tāmen shū le.

他們輸了。

The two teams are even.

Liǎng duì píngshǒu.

兩隊平手。

Word Bank 61 Sporting facilities

fitness center	▶ jiànshēnfáng	健身房
playground	▶ cāochǎng	操場
stadium	▶ tǐyùchǎng	體育場
swimming pool	▶ yóuyǒngchí	游泳池
tennis court	▶ wǎngqiúchǎng	網球場
weightlifting room	▶ jǔzhòngshì	舉重室

Note 12

In naming a sporting venue, Chinese is much easier than English. All you have to do is to put the suffix "——chǎng," which means literally "a field," after the sport, be it a "court," "course," or "field" in English. Thus, a "tennis court" is "wǎngqiúchǎng," while a "golf course" is "gāo'ěrfūqiúchǎng," etc.

ENTERTAINMENT

3 *By the Waterfront*

I'd like to try windsurfing.

Wǒ xiǎng shìshi fānbǎn.
我想試試帆板。

How much do you charge then?

Fèiyong zěnme suàn?
費用怎麼算？

US$20 per hour.

Yì xiǎoshí èrshí kuài měijīn.
一小時二十塊美金。

RMB400 per day.

Yì tiān sìbǎi kuài rénmínbì.
一天四百塊人民幣。

Do I need to be experienced?

Yídìng yào yǒu jīngyàn cái xíng ma?
一定要有經驗才行嗎？

Yes, experience is a must.

Duì, yídìng yào yǒu jīngyàn.
對，一定要有經驗。

No, you do not need to be experienced.

Bù, búbì yǒu jīngyàn.
不，不必有經驗。

You need to take the introductory course.

Nǐ děi xiān shàng shuōmíng kèchéng.
你得先上說明課程。

I'd like to take the beginner's course.

Wǒ xiǎng shàng chūjí kèchéng.
我想上初級課程。

Word Bank 62 Waterfront sports

cruise	yóutǐng chūyóu	遊艇出遊
fishing	diàoyú	釣魚
jet skiing	shuǐshàng mótuōtǐng	水上摩托艇
	shuǐshàng mótuōchē	水上摩托車
rafting	píhuátǐng	皮划艇
	piāoliú	漂流
	fànzhōu	泛舟
sailing	fānchuán chūyóu	帆船出遊
scuba diving	shuǐfèi qiánshuǐ	水肺潛水
snorkeling	qiánshuǐ	潛水
	fúqián	浮潛
surfing	chōnglàng	衝浪
water-skiing	huáshuǐ	滑水

ENTERTAINMENT

239

We offer free instruction.

Wǒmen tígōng miǎnfèi zhǐdǎo.

我們提供免費指導。

What's the weather going to be like tomorrow?

Míngtiān tiānqì zěnmeyàng?

明天天氣怎麼樣？

I'd like to make a reservation for tomorrow's course.

Wǒ yào yùyuē míngtiān de kèchéng.

我要預約明天的課程。

What time do we start?

Jǐ diǎn kāishǐ?

幾點開始？

How long does it take?

Yào duōjiǔ shíjiān?

要多久時間？

Can I rent the equipment here?

Zū de dào zhuāngbèi ma?

租得到裝備嗎？

You can go to the counter over there to rent the equipment.

Nàge guìtái kěyǐ zū zhuāngbèi.

那個櫃檯可以租裝備。

Please show me how to use the equipment.

Qǐng jiāo wǒ zěnyàng shǐyòng zhuāngbèi.

請教我怎樣使用裝備。

Is it far to the beach?

Dào shātān qù yuǎn bu yuǎn?

到沙灘去遠不遠？

Word Bank 63 Equipments for waterfront sports

beach umbrella	▶ zhēyángsǎn	遮陽傘
boat	▶ chuán	船
chair	▶ yǐzi	椅子
fishing rod	▶ diàogān	釣竿
life jacket	▶ jiùshēngyī	救生衣
locker	▶ cúnbāoguì ▶ jìwùguì	存包櫃 寄物櫃
snorkel	▶ hūxīguǎnr	呼吸管兒
surfboard	▶ chōnglàngbǎn	衝浪板
towel	▶ máojīn	毛巾
wetsuit	▶ qiánshuǐ-zhuāng	潛水裝

ENTERTAINMENT

The riverbank is not far away.

Zhèr lí hébiān bú tài yuǎn.

這兒離河邊不太遠。

Where do I change clothes?

Nǎr kěyǐ huàn yīfu?

哪兒可以換衣服？

Can I swim there?

Nàr kěyǐ yóuyǒng ma?

那兒可以游泳嗎？

Can I take a shower here?

Kěyǐ zài zhèr línyù ma?

可以在這兒淋浴嗎？

Swimming is prohibited.

Jìnzhǐ yóuyǒng.

禁止游泳。

When's the high tide?

Shénme shíhou zhǎngcháo?

什麼時候漲潮？

What time is the low tide?

Jǐ diǎn tuìcháo?

幾點退潮？

Is it deep here?

Zhèr de shuǐ shēn ma?

這兒的水深嗎？

What's the water temperature?

Shuǐwēn jǐ dù?

水溫幾度？

It's 15 degrees Celsius.

Shuǐwēn shì Shèshì shíwǔ dù.

水溫是攝氏十五度。

Do You Know? ㉓ **Fahrenheit vs. Celsius**

°F (Fahrenheit degree) = (9/5 × °C) + 32
°C (Celsius degree) = (°F − 32) × 5/9
So 15 °C is equal to 59 °F.

4 *At a Night Club*

I heard that you have the best jazz club in town.

Tīngshuō nǐmen shì běndì zuì hǎo de juéshì jiǔbā.

聽說你們是本地最好的爵士酒吧。

What performance do you have for tonight?

Jīntiān wǎnshang yǒu shénme biǎoyǎn?

今天晚上有什麼表演？

We have a saxophone performance.

Yǒu yì chǎng sàkèsīguǎnr yǎnzòu.

有一場薩克斯管兒演奏。

Word Bank 64 Fun places

casino	dǔchǎng	賭場
gay/lesbian bar	tóngxìngliàn jùlèbù / tóngzhì jiǔbā	同性戀俱樂部 同志酒吧
karaoke	kǎlā OK	卡拉 OK
lounge bar	jiǔláng	酒廊
night club	yèzǒnghuì	夜總會
piano bar	gāngqín jiǔbā	鋼琴酒吧
pub	jiǔguǎn	酒館

Is a reservation necessary?

Xūyào yùdìng ma?

需要預訂嗎？

We have the best cocktails.

Wǒmen de jīwěijiǔ hěn bàng.

我們的雞尾酒很棒。

How much do you charge for the night?

Fèiyong zěnme suàn?

費用怎麼算？

US$20 per person.

Yí ge rén èrshí kuài měijīn.

一個人二十塊美金。

A drink is included.

Fùsòng yǐnliào.

附送飲料。

Food is excluded.

Bú fù cāndiǎn.

不附餐點。

When is the first set?

Dì-yī chǎng shì shénme shíhou?

第一場是什麼時候？

What time does the last show start?

Zuìhòu yì chǎng jǐ diǎn kāishǐ?

最後一場幾點開始？

I'd like a good table.

Qǐng gěi wǒ xuǎn yì zhāng hǎo zhuōzi.

請給我選一張好桌子。

Do you take requests?

Kěyǐ diǎn gē ma?

可以點歌嗎？

Do you have any minimum charge?

Yǒu méiyǒu zuìdī xiāofèi?

有沒有最低消費？

Is there a dress code?

Fúzhuāng yǒu méiyǒu guīdìng?

服裝有沒有規定？

Could you change the ashtray?

Néng tì wǒ huàn yānhuīgāng ma?

能替我換煙灰缸嗎？

When are you closing tonight?

Jǐ diǎn dǎyàng?

幾點打烊？

We are closing at 12:00.

Shí'èr diǎn dǎyàng.

十二點打烊。

Word Bank 65 Performances

alternative rock	lìnglèi yáogǔn	另類搖滾
dance	wǔdǎo	舞蹈
drag queen show	fǎnchuànxiù	反串秀
folk music	míngē	民歌
guitar	jítā	吉他
jazz	juéshìyuè	爵士樂
live band	xiànchǎng yǎnzòu	現場演奏
oldie	liúxíng lǎogē	流行老歌
piano	gāngqín	鋼琴
pop music	liúxíng yīnyuè	流行音樂
rock 'n' roll	yáogǔnyuè	搖滾樂
saxophone	sàkèsīguǎnr sàkèsīfēng	薩克斯管兒 薩克斯風
vocal performance	yǎnchàng	演唱

Note 13

In this part of the world, many categories of music are named either in Chinese with a phonetic translation from English, or in English. For instance, R & B is simply R & B while Funk is "fāngkè" or Funk. So don't bother to find the Chinese translations if you don't have any idea. Just say them in English, and you will be perfectly understood.

Notes

Trouble

1 Lost Items

Can you tell me where the lost-and-found is?

Qǐngwèn, shīwù zhāolǐngchù zài nǎr?

請問，失物招領處在哪兒？

I have lost my wallet.

Wǒ de qiánbāo bújiàn le.

我的錢包不見了。

Could you help me look for my wallet?

Nǐ kěyǐ bāng wǒ zhǎo qiánbāo ma?

你可以幫我找錢包嗎？

Could you announce it for me?

Nǐ kěyǐ bāng wǒ guǎngbō ma?

你可以幫我廣播嗎？

Word Bank 66 Personal belongings

backpack	▶ bèibāo	背包
book	▶ shū	書
camcorder	▶ shèxiàngjī	攝像機
	▶ shèyǐngjī	攝影機
camera	▶ zhàoxiàngjī	照相機
CD player	▶ suíshēntīng	隨身聽

cell phone	▶ shǒujī	手機
credit card	▶ xìnyòngkǎ	信用卡
data	▶ zīliào	資料
driver's license	▶ jiàzhào	駕照
glasses	▶ yǎnjìng	眼鏡
hat	▶ màozi	帽子
jacket	▶ wàitào	外套
keys	▶ yàoshi	鑰匙
luggage	▶ xíngli	行李
map	▶ dìtú	地圖
money	▶ qián	錢
notebook	▶ bǐjìběn	筆記本
passport	▶ hùzhào	護照
pen	▶ bǐ	筆
permission	▶ xǔkězhèng	許可證
plane ticket	▶ jīpiào	機票
purse/wallet	▶ qiánbāo	錢包
raincoat	▶ yǔyī	雨衣
train ticket	▶ huǒchēpiào	火車票
umbrella	▶ yǔsǎn	雨傘

TROUBLE

Have you seen a suitcase around here?

Yǒu méiyǒu kàndào yí ge shǒutíxiāng?
有沒有看到一個手提箱？

What kind of suitcase is it?

Shì shénmeyàng de shǒutíxiāng?
是什麼樣的手提箱？

It is about this size.

Chàbuduō zhème dà.
差不多這麼大。

It's blue.

Lánsè de.
藍色的。 see p.167

Where did you leave it just now?

Gāngcái fàng zài nǎr?
剛才放在哪兒？

I left it on the table.

Fàng zài zhuōzi shang.
放在桌子上。

Where did you lose it?

Nǐ zài nǎr diū de?
你在哪兒丟的？

I lost it on the bus.

Wǒ zài gōngjiāochē shang diū de.
我在公交車上丟的。

I don't know where I lost it.

Wǒ bù zhīdao zài nǎli diū de.

我不知道在哪裡丟的。

Word Bank 67 Places where you might leave your stuff at / on

airplane	▶ fēijī shang	飛機上
airport	▶ fēijīchǎng	飛機場
bus stop	▶ gōngjiāozhàn	公交站
	▶ gōngchēzhàn	公車站
here	▶ zhèli	這裡
lobby	▶ dàtīng	大廳
movie theater	▶ diànyǐngyuàn	電影院
park	▶ gōngyuán	公園
railroad station	▶ huǒchēzhàn	火車站
restaurant	▶ fànguǎn	飯館
restroom	▶ wèishēngjiān	衛生間
	▶ xǐshǒujiān	洗手間
subway	▶ dìtiě shang	地鐵上
subway station	▶ dìtiězhàn	地鐵站
taxi	▶ chūzūchē	出租車
	▶ jìchéngchē	計程車
there	▶ nàli	那裡
train	▶ huǒchē shang	火車上

TROUBLE

When did you lose it?

Nǐ shénme shíhou diū de?

你什麼時候丟的？

I lost it just now.

Gāngcái diū de.

剛才丟的。 see pp.24-27, 33

What's inside?

Lǐmian yǒu shénme dōngxi?

裡面有什麼東西？

My passport is inside.

Lǐmian yǒu hùzhào.

裡面有護照。

You can ask at the lost-and-found.

Nǐ kěyǐ qù shīwù zhāolǐngchù wènwen.

你可以去失物招領處問問。

Is this yours?

Zhèige shì bu shì nǐ de?

這個是不是你的？

Yes, it is. Thank you.

Shìde. Xièxie nǐ.

是的。謝謝你。

I am here to collect my passport.

Wǒ yào lǐnghui wǒ de hùzhào.

我要領回我的護照。

Please proceed to window number 3.

Qǐng dào sān hào chuāngkǒu.

請到三號窗口。

Can I collect it tomorrow?

Wǒ míngtiān kěyǐ nádào ma?

我明天可以拿到嗎？

Please call me if you find it.

Rúguǒ zhǎodào le, qǐng dǎ diànhuà gěi wǒ.

如果找到了，請打電話給我。

Word Bank 68 Helpful places you can seek

bank	▶ yínháng	銀行
embassy	▶ dàshǐguǎn	大使館
fire station	▶ xiāofángduì	消防隊
hospital	▶ yīyuàn	醫院
information table	▶ fúwùtái	服務台
insurance company	▶ bǎoxiǎn gōngsī	保險公司
lost-and-found	▶ shīwù zhāolǐngchù	失物招領處
pharmacy	▶ yàofáng	藥房
police station	▶ jǐngchájú	警察局
repair shop	▶ xiūchēchǎng	修車廠

TROUBLE

2 *Robbery & Scams*

Be careful!

Xiǎoxīn!

小心！

Grab him!

Zhuāzhù tā!

抓住他！

My camera has been stolen.

Wǒ de zhàoxiàngjī bèi tōu le!

我的照相機被偷了！

I have been cheated.

Wǒ bèi piàn le.

我被騙了。

I have been robbed.

Wǒ bèi qiǎng le.

我被搶了。

Where did you get robbed?

Nǐ zài nǎr bèi qiǎng de?

你在哪兒被搶的？

At the railroad station.

Zài huǒchēzhàn.

在火車站。

Word Bank 69 Wrongdoings

attack	▶ gōngjī	攻擊
beat up	▶ dǎshāng	打傷
cheat	▶ piàn	騙
harass	▶ sāorǎo	騷擾
pickpocket	▶ pá	扒
rape	▶ qiángjiān	強姦
rob	▶ qiǎng	搶
steal	▶ tōu	偷
trail	▶ gēnzōng	跟蹤

Word Bank 70 Wrongdoers

fake beggar	▶ jiǎ qǐgài	假乞丐
fake police	▶ jiǎ jǐngchá	假警察
hooligan	▶ liúmáng	流氓
pickpocket	▶ páshǒu	扒手
robber	▶ qiángdào	強盜
swindler	▶ piànzi	騙子
thief	▶ xiǎotōu	小偷

TROUBLE

How much money did the robber steal from you?

Nǐ bèi qiǎngle duōshao qián?

你被搶了多少錢？

About 500 dollars.

Dàgài wǔbǎi kuài qián.

大概五百塊錢。

What I bought was a forgery.

Wǒ mǎidào jiǎhuò le.

我買到假貨了。

This bill is a counterfeit.

Zhè shì jiǎchāo.

這是假鈔。

Show me your Police ID.

Wǒ yào kàn nǐ de jǐngcházhèng.

我要看你的警察證。

Word Bank 71 Calling for help

Call an ambulance!	▶ Jiào jiùhùchē!	叫救護車！
Call the police!	▶ Jiào jǐngchá!	叫警察！
Get out quickly!	▶ Kuài chūqu!	快出去！
Help!	▶ Jiùmìng a!	救命啊！
Take me to the hospital!	▶ Sòng wǒ qù yīyuàn!	送我去醫院！

TROUBLE

3 Injury

I am injured.

Wǒ shòushāng le.

我受傷了。

My hand is bleeding.

Wǒ de shǒu liúxuè le.

我的手流血了。

I have sprained my ankle.

Wǒ de jiǎo niǔ le.

我的腳扭了。

I've got a cramp.

Wǒ chōujīn le.

我抽筋了。

I fell over.

Wǒ shuāidǎo le.

我摔倒了。

I have been bitten by a snake.

Wǒ bèi shé yǎo le.

我被蛇咬了。

He hit his head and it swelled up.

Tā de tóu zhǒng le.

他的頭腫了。

He fainted.

Tā hūndǎo le.
他昏倒了。

I have been knocked down.

Wǒ bèi chē zhuàng le.
我被車撞了。

I have had a car accident.

Wǒ fāshēngle chēhuò.
我發生了車禍。

Word Bank 72 Harmful animals and insects

ant	▶ mǎyǐ	螞蟻
cockroach	▶ zhāngláng	蟑螂
mosquito	▶ wénzi	蚊子
mouse	▶ lǎoshǔ	老鼠
scorpion	▶ xiēzi	蠍子
snake	▶ shé	蛇
spider	▶ zhīzhū	蜘蛛
street cat	▶ yěmāo	野貓
street dog	▶ yěgǒu	野狗
wasp	▶ huángfēng	黃蜂

Is it serious?

Yánzhòng bù yánzhòng?

嚴重不嚴重？

It's okay. It's not that serious.

Hái hǎo. Bú tài yánzhòng.

還好。不太嚴重。

Please support me for a moment.

Qǐng nǐ fú wǒ yíxià.

請你扶我一下。

He needs an emergency treatment.

Tā xūyào jíjiù.

他需要急救。

I need to go to the hospital.

Wǒ xūyào qù yīyuàn.

我需要去醫院。

I need a wheelchair.

Wǒ xūyào lúnyǐ.

我需要輪椅。

Please help me to stop the bleeding.

Qǐng bāng wǒ zhǐxiě.

請幫我止血。

Please help me to dress the wound.

Qǐng bāng wǒ bāozā.

請幫我包紮。

Word Bank 73 Injuries

English	Pinyin	Chinese
abrasion	cāshāng	擦傷
bleed	liúxuè	流血
burn (by fire)	shāoshāng	燒傷
burn (by hot water)	tàngshāng	燙傷
concussion	nǎozhèndàng	腦震盪
cramp	chōujīn	抽筋
cut	gēshāng	割傷
dislocation	tuōjiù	脫臼
excessive loss of blood	shīxuè guòduō	失血過多
faint	hūndǎo	昏倒
fracture	gǔzhé	骨折
inflame	fāyán	發炎
internal bleeding	nèichūxuè	內出血
knock down	zhuàngshāng	撞傷
poisoning	zhòngdú	中毒
pull	lāshāng	拉傷
puncture wound	cìshāng	刺傷
raw	cāpò pí	擦破皮
sprain	niǔshāng	扭傷
swell	zhǒng qilai	腫起來

TROUBLE

4 *Sickness*

What's wrong?

Nǐ nǎr bù shūfu?

你哪兒不舒服？

I have got a serious headache.

Wǒ de tóu hěn tòng.

我的頭很痛。

Word Bank 74 How do you feel?

cold	hěn lěng	很冷
drowsy	hūnhūn-chénchén de	昏昏沉沉的
headache	tóutòng	頭痛
nausea	xiǎng tù	想吐
numb	mámá de	麻麻的
sore throat	hóulongtòng	喉嚨痛
stabbing pain	hěn tòng	很痛
stomachache	wèitòng	胃痛
toothache	yátòng	牙痛
uncomfortable	hěn nánguò	很難過
weak	méiyǒu lìqi	沒有力氣

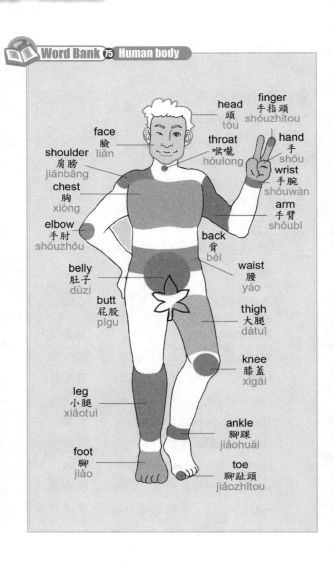

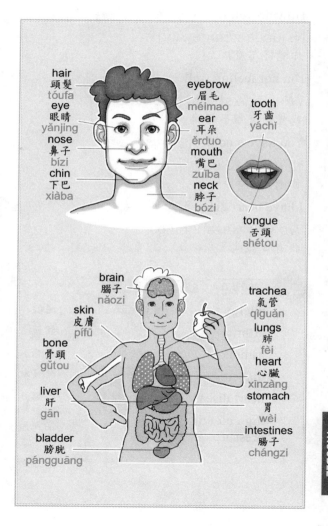

hair
頭髮
tóufa

eye
眼睛
yǎnjing

nose
鼻子
bízi

chin
下巴
xiàba

eyebrow
眉毛
méimao

ear
耳朵
ěrduo

mouth
嘴巴
zuǐba

neck
脖子
bózi

tooth
牙齒
yáchǐ

tongue
舌頭
shétou

brain
腦子
nǎozi

skin
皮膚
pífū

bone
骨頭
gǔtou

liver
肝
gān

bladder
膀胱
pángguāng

trachea
氣管
qìguǎn

lungs
肺
fèi

heart
心臟
xīnzàng

stomach
胃
wèi

intestines
腸子
chángzi

TROUBLE

How do you feel?

Nǐ juéde zěnmeyàng?

你覺得怎麼樣？

I'm not feeling well.

Wǒ juéde shēntǐ bù shūfu.

我覺得身體不舒服。

You have a cold.

Nǐ gǎnmào le.

你感冒了。

I have heart disease.

Wǒ yǒu xīnzàngbìng.

我有心臟病。

Word Bank 76 Clinical illness

allergy	▶ guòmǐn	過敏
arthritis	▶ guānjiéyán	關節炎
asthma	▶ qìchuǎn	氣喘
diabetes	▶ tángniàobìng	糖尿病
heart disease	▶ xīnzàngbìng	心臟病
high blood pressure	▶ gāoxuèyā	高血壓

TROUBLE

You should go to a doctor.

Nǐ yīnggāi qù kàn yīshēng.

你應該去看醫生。

Please take me to the hospital.

Qǐng sòng wǒ qù yīyuàn.

請送我去醫院。

You should get plenty of rest.

Nǐ xūyào duō xiūxi.

你需要多休息。

I want some water.

Wǒ yào hē shuǐ.

我要喝水。

Can you walk?

Nǐ hái zǒu de dòng ma?

你還走得動嗎？

I can't walk anymore.

Wǒ zǒu bú dòng le.

我走不動了。

I have some medicine.

Wǒ yǒu yào.

我有藥。

Please pass me the medicine.

Qǐng bǎ yào ná gěi wǒ.

請把藥拿給我。

TROUBLE

267

Is the problem serious?

Nǐ de bìng yánzhòng ma?
你的病嚴重嗎？

I don't think it's serious.

Wǒ juéde bú tài yánzhòng.
我覺得不太嚴重。

Is there a doctor who understands English?

Yǒu méiyǒu huì shuō Yīngyǔ de yīshēng?
有沒有會說英語的醫生？

Word Bank 77 Symptoms

airsickness	▶ yùnjī	暈機
carsickness	▶ yùnchē	暈車
cold	▶ gǎnmào	感冒
constipation	▶ biànmì	便祕
cough	▶ késou	咳嗽
diarrhea	▶ lādùzi	拉肚子
fever	▶ fāshāo	發燒
running nose	▶ liúbíshuǐ	流鼻水
seasickness	▶ yùnchuán	暈船
shock	▶ xiūkè	休克
shuddering	▶ fādǒu	發抖
sunstroke	▶ zhòngshǔ	中暑

TROUBLE

5 *Seeing a Doctor*

I want to go to the emergency room.

Wǒ yào kàn jízhěn.

我要看急診。

Where do I register?

Zài nǎr guàhào?

在哪兒掛號？

Please take your clothes off.

Qǐng tuōxia yīfu.

請脫下衣服。

Please lie down.

Qǐng tǎng xialai.

請躺下來。

Please open your mouth.

Qǐng zhāngkai zuǐba.

請張開嘴巴。

You need to be hospitalized.

Nǐ xūyào zhùyuàn.

你需要住院。

Please give me a proof of the diagnosis.

Qǐng gěi wǒ zhěnduàn zhèngmíng.

請給我診斷證明。

TROUBLE

Please notify the insurance company.

Qǐng tōngzhī bǎoxiǎn gōngsī.

請通知保險公司。

Do you have any drug allergies?

Nǐ yǒu méiyǒu yàowù guòmǐn?

你有沒有藥物過敏？

I am allergic to aspirin.

Wǒ duì āsīpǐlín guòmǐn.

我對阿斯匹林過敏。

This is the prescription.

Zhè shì yàodān.

這是藥單。

Word Bank 78 Medical treatments

get a blood test	chōuxuè	抽血
give an injection	dǎzhēn	打針
have an X-ray examination	zhào X-guāng	照 X 光
lie down	tǎngxia	躺下
take blood pressure	liáng xuèyā	量血壓
take temperature	liáng tǐwēn	量體溫
to be hospitalized	zhùyuàn	住院
undergo an operation	kāidāo	開刀

TROUBLE

6 *Buying Medicine*

I want to buy medicine for a cold.

Wǒ yào mǎi gǎnmàoyào.

我要買感冒藥。

Please buy some medicine for me.

Qǐng bāng wǒ mǎi yào.

請幫我買藥。

(Show the package) I'd like to have some of this medicine.

Wǒ mǎi zhè zhǒng yào.

我買這種藥。

How many times a day should I take this medicine?

Zhè zhǒng yào yì tiān chī jǐ cì?

這種藥一天吃幾次？

Take this medicine three times a day.

Zhè zhǒng yào yì tiān chī sān cì.

這種藥一天吃三次。

Before or after meals?

Fànqián chī huò fànhòu chī?

飯前吃或飯後吃？

Take one dose after meals.

Fànhòu chī yì bāo.

飯後吃一包。

Take one dose before bed.

Shuìqián chī yì bāo.

睡前吃一包。

Word Bank 79 Medicine

anti-diarrhea	▶ zhǐxièyào	止瀉藥
aspirin	▶ āsīpǐlín	阿斯匹林
	▶ āsīpǐlíng	阿斯匹靈
asthma medicine	▶ qìchuǎnyào	氣喘藥
carsickness medicine	▶ yùnchēyào	暈車藥
heart disease medicine	▶ xīnzàngbìng yào	心臟病藥
high blood pressure medicine	▶ jiàng xuèyā yào	降血壓藥
medicine for a cold	▶ gǎnmàoyào	感冒藥
pain killer	▶ zhǐtòngyào	止痛藥
throat drop	▶ hóutáng	喉糖

What are the side effects?

Yǒu méiyǒu fùzuòyòng?

有沒有副作用？

This is for external use only.

Zhè shì wàiyòngyào.

這是外用藥。

 Word Bank 80 Health care products

anti-fungus ointment	▶ qùxuǎn yàogāo	去癬藥膏
condom	▶ bìyùntào ▶ bǎoxiǎntào	避孕套 保險套
contact lenses cleaning solution	yǐnxíng yǎnjìng ▶ chōngxǐ yàoshuǐ	隱形眼鏡 沖洗藥水
contact lenses disinfecting solution	yǐnxíng yǎnjìng ▶ xiāodú yàoshuǐ	隱形眼鏡 消毒藥水
eye drops	▶ yǎnyàoshuǐ	眼藥水
fabric bandage	▶ bēngdài	繃帶
first aid adhesive bandage	▶ chuāngkětiē ▶ OK bēng	創可貼 OK 繃

TROUBLE

273

green oil	▶ lǜyóujīng	綠油精
lip balm	▶ chúngāo	唇膏
	▶ hùchúngāo	護唇膏
mouthwash	▶ shùkǒushuǐ	漱口水
palm oil	▶ wànjīnyóu	萬金油
sanitary towel	▶ wèishēngjīn	衛生巾
	▶ wèishēngmián	衛生棉
suntan lotion	▶ fángshàiyóu	防晒油
swab	▶ shābù	紗布
talcum powder	▶ fèizifěn	痱子粉

7 *Breakdowns & Repairs*

My camera is broken.

Wǒ de zhàoxiàngjī huài le.

我的照相機壞了。

My backpack is damaged.

Wǒ de bèibāo pò le.

我的背包破了。

Can you fix it?

Nǐ kěyǐ xiūlǐ ma?

你可以修理嗎？

My car has broken down.

Wǒ de chē huài le.

我的車壞了。

Can you change the tire for me?

Nǐ kěyǐ bāng wǒ huàn lúntāi ma?

你可以幫我換輪胎嗎？

My car battery is dead.

Wǒ de chē méi diàn le.

我的車沒電了。

Can you recharge the battery for me?

Nǐ kěyǐ bāng wǒ chōngdiàn ma?

你可以幫我充電嗎？

My car needs to be towed.

Wǒ de chē xūyào tuōdiào.

我的車需要拖吊。

Please contact the insurance company for me.

Qǐng bāng wǒ liánluò bǎoxiǎn gōngsī.

請幫我聯絡保險公司。

Please call me a tow truck.

Qǐng bāng wǒ jiào tuōdiàochē.

請幫我叫拖吊車。

Word Bank 81 Car problems

air conditioner not working	kōngtiáo huài le	空調壞了
brakes broken	shāchē huài le	煞車壞了
broken windshield wiper	yǔshuā huài le	雨刷壞了
defective seat belt	ānquándài huài le	安全帶壞了
flat tire	lúntāi méi qì	輪胎沒氣
headlights not working	dàdēng bú liàng	大燈不亮
horn broken	lǎba huài le	喇叭壞了

TROUBLE

indicator lights not working	▶ fāngxiàngdēng bú liàng	方向燈不亮
leakage of water tank	▶ shuǐxiāng lòushuǐ	水箱漏水
unable to start	▶ fādòng bùliǎo	發動不了

Notes

8 *Troubles on the Road*

There has been a fire. We are not able to get through.

Nàli fāshēng huǒzāi, wǒmen guò bu qù.

那裡發生火災，我們過不去。

There has been a car accident.

Nàli fāshēng chēhuò.

那裡發生車禍。

The road is blocked.

Nà tiáo lù bù tōng.

那條路不通。

This road is slippery.

Zhèi tiáo lù hěn huá.

這條路很滑。

We are going to cancel our trip.

Wǒmen yào qǔxiāo lǚxíng jìhuà.

我們要取消旅行計劃。

It's very dangerous here.

Zhèli hěn wēixiǎn.

這裡很危險。

Walk slowly.

Mànmàn zǒu.

慢慢走。

Watch out for falling stones.

Xiǎoxīn luòshí.

小心落石。

Watch out for falling stuff.

Xiǎoxīn dōngxi diào xialai.

小心東西掉下來。

Word Bank 62 Road situations

foggy	▶ yǒu wù	有霧
heavy rain	▶ xià dàyǔ	下大雨
heavy snowfall	▶ xià dàxuě	下大雪
holes in the road	▶ lùshang yǒu kēngdòng	路上有坑洞
landslide up ahead	▶ qiánmian tāfāng	前面塌方
	▶ qiánmian tānfāng	前面坍方
no entry	▶ jìnzhǐ tōngxíng	禁止通行
road repairs up ahead	▶ qiánmian xiūlù	前面修路
traffic jam	▶ dǔchē	堵車
	▶ sāichē	塞車

TROUBLE

Don't get closer.

Búyào kàojìn.

不要靠近。

Don't go there.

Búyào guòqu.

不要過去。

There are a lot of earthquakes here. Please watch out.

Zhèli cháng yǒu dìzhèn. Qǐng xiǎoxīn.

這裡常有地震。請小心。

Fires and BBQs are prohibited here.

Zhèli jìnzhǐ shēnghuǒ, kǎoròu.

這裡禁止生火、烤肉。

Please do not smoke here.

Qǐng bú yào zài zhèli xīyān.

請不要在這裡吸煙。

The river is too deep. We can not go over.

Héshuǐ tài shēn, wǒmen guò bu qù.

河水太深，我們過不去。

TROUBLE

Word Bank 83 Natural disasters

drought	▶ hànzāi	旱災
earthquake	▶ dìzhèn	地震
explosion	▶ bàozhà	爆炸
fire	▶ huǒzāi	火災
flood	▶ shuǐzāi	水災
landslide	▶ tāfāng	塌方
	▶ tānfāng	坍方
tsunami	▶ hǎixiào	海嘯
typhoon	▶ táifēng	颱風

Notes

Menu & Shopping List

Menu

Chinese Cuisine

Rice & noodles

pork & pickled mustard green noodles	▶ zhàcài ròusī miàn	榨菜肉絲麵
hot beef noodles soup	▶ hóngshāo niúròu miàn	紅燒牛肉麵
noodles with meat sauce	▶ zhájiàngmiàn	炸醬麵
noodles with gravy	▶ dàlǔmiàn	大滷麵
noodles with shredded chicken	▶ jīsīmiàn	雞絲麵
Cantonese style pan fried noodles	▶ guǎngzhōu chǎomiàn	廣州炒麵
shijin fried noodles	▶ shíjǐn chǎomiàn	什錦炒麵
pork ribs noodle soup	▶ páigǔmiàn	排骨麵
sliced noodles	▶ dāoxiāomiàn	刀削麵
minced meat noodles	▶ ròujiàngmiàn	肉醬麵
ham fried rice	▶ huǒtuǐ dàn chǎofàn	火腿蛋炒飯

shrimp fried rice	▶ xiārén dàn chǎofàn	蝦仁蛋炒飯
Yangzhou fried rice	▶ yángzhōu chǎofàn	揚州炒飯
beef stewed with rice	▶ niúnǎnfàn	牛腩飯
curry rice	▶ gālífàn	咖喱飯
chicken leg with rice	▶ jītuǐfàn	雞腿飯
fried fish fillet with rice	▶ yúpáifàn	魚排飯
meat sauce with rice	▶ lǔròufàn	滷肉飯

Pork

steamed pork with salted dried mustard cabbage	▶ méigān-kòuròu	梅干扣肉
spareribs with black bean sauce	▶ chǐzhī-páigǔ	豉汁排骨
steamed spareribs	▶ fěnzhēng-páigǔ	粉蒸排骨
omelet with shredded pork	▶ mùxiròu	木樨肉
fried sliced pork with brown sauce	▶ jiàngbàoròu	醬爆肉
sweet & sour pork	▶ tángcù-lǐjí	糖醋里脊
pork meat balls	▶ shīzitóu	獅子頭

Dongpo-style stewed pork	▶ dōngpōròu	東坡肉
honeyed ham	▶ mìzhī-huǒtuǐ	蜜汁火腿
boiled pork with garlic sauce	▶ suànní-báiròu	蒜泥白肉
bitter gourd stuffed with meat	▶ kǔguā-xiāngròu	苦瓜鑲肉
roasted pig's intestine	▶ jiǔzhuǎn-féicháng	九轉肥腸
garlic-fried sausage	▶ suànbào-xiāngcháng	蒜爆香腸

Beef

stir fried beef with green pepper	▶ qīngjiāo-ròusī	青椒肉絲
stir fried beef with onions	▶ yángcōng-niúliǔ	洋蔥牛柳
grilled beef	▶ tiěpá-niúròu	鐵扒牛肉
stir fried beef with oyster sauce	▶ háoyóu-niúròu	蠔油牛肉
beef with broccoli	▶ gàilán-niúròu	芥藍牛肉
fried beef with scramble eggs	▶ huádàn-niúròu	滑蛋牛肉
beef on skewer	▶ chuànshāo-niúpái	串燒牛排
Mongolian barbecue	▶ ménggǔ-kǎoròu	蒙古烤肉
fried tripe	▶ bàoniúdǔ	爆牛肚

Poultry & eggs

Kung Pao chicken	▶ gōngbǎo-jīdīng	宮保雞丁
steamed chicken	▶ báizhǎnjī	白斬雞
curry chicken	▶ gālíjī	咖喱雞
boiled chicken with scallion and oil	▶ cōngyóujī	蔥油雞
braised chicken	▶ mènjī	燜雞
stir fried chicken in wine sauce	▶ xiāngzāo-jīpiàn	香糟雞片
air-pot chicken	▶ qìguōjī	汽鍋雞
3 cup chicken Taiwan style	▶ sānbēijī	三杯雞
Beijing duck	▶ běijīng-kǎoyā	北京烤鴨
scrambled egg with tomatoes	▶ fānqié-chǎodàn	番茄炒蛋
baked egg with onions	▶ yángcōng-hōngdàn	洋蔥烘蛋
fried egg	▶ hébāodàn	荷包蛋

Seafood

sweet & sour fish	▶ tángcùyú	糖醋魚
stewed carp with hot bean sauce	▶ dòubànyú	豆瓣魚
cod with soybean crumb	▶ dòusū-xuěyú	豆酥鱈魚

stewed fish head with brown sauce in casserole	▶ yútóu-shāguō	魚頭砂鍋
baked egg with prawns	▶ xiārén-hōngdàn	蝦仁烘蛋
stir fried shrimp with cashew nuts	▶ yāoguǒ-xiārén	腰果蝦仁
deep fried prawn	▶ chǎomíngxiā	炒明蝦
stir fried shrimp with pineapple	▶ fènglí-xiāqiú	鳳梨蝦球
hairy crab (river crab)	▶ dàzháxiè	大閘蟹
shark's fin with mushrooms, bamboo shoots & chicken shreds	▶ sānsī-yúchì	三絲魚翅
braised sea cucumber with spring onions	▶ cōngshāo-hǎishēn	蔥燒海參
sliced abalone in oyster sauce	▶ háoyóu-pá-bàoyú	蠔油扒鮑魚

Tofu & other vegetables

fried tofu	▶ zhá dòufu	炸豆腐
Mapo tofu	▶ mápó-dòufu	麻婆豆腐
tofu with brown sauce	▶ hóngshāo dòufu	紅燒豆腐

preserved egg mixed tofu	▶ pídàn dòufu	皮蛋豆腐
tofu salad	▶ liángbàn dòufu	涼拌豆腐
cabbage with dried shrimps	▶ shàngtāng-báicài	上湯白菜
stir fried bean sprout	▶ chǎodòuyá	炒豆芽
stir fried bamboo shoots with mushrooms	▶ chǎoshuāngdōng	炒雙冬
pickled mustard green with bean curd leaf	▶ xuěcài-bǎiyè	雪菜百葉

Soup

double boiled supreme seafood & meat	▶ fótiàoqiáng	佛跳牆
borsch	▶ luósòngtāng	羅宋湯
vegetable & bean curd soup	▶ qīngcài dòufu tāng	青菜豆腐湯
clam soup	▶ gélítāng	蛤蜊湯
hot & sour soup	▶ suānlàtāng	酸辣湯
egg drop soup	▶ dànhuātāng	蛋花湯
fish ball soup	▶ yúwántāng	魚丸湯
meat ball soup	▶ gòngwántāng	貢丸湯
wonton soup	▶ húntuntāng	餛飩湯

bitter gourd spareribs soup	▶ kǔguā páigǔ tāng	苦瓜排骨湯
crab meat & corn soup	▶ xièròu yùmǐ tāng	蟹肉玉米湯
chicken & corn soup	▶ jīróng yùmǐ tāng	雞茸玉米湯
mushroom soup	▶ mógu tāng	蘑菇湯

Local snacks

oyster thin noodles	▶ ézǎi miànxiàn	蚵仔麵線
fried rice noodles	▶ chǎomǐfěn	炒米粉
squid thick soup	▶ yóuyúgēng	魷魚羹
fermented tofu	▶ chòudòufu	臭豆腐
corn bread	▶ wōwotóu	窩窩頭
sponge cake	▶ fāgāo	發糕
stewed mix meat	▶ lǔwèi	滷味
crispy salty chicken	▶ xiánsūjī	鹹酥雞
spring roll	▶ chūnjuǎn	春捲
pancake	▶ dàbǐng	大餅
Taiwanese-style rice cake	▶ wǎnguǒ	碗粿
moon cake	▶ yuèbǐng	月餅
glutinous rice cake	▶ niángāo	年糕
glutinous rice dumpling	▶ zòngzi	粽子

crispy rice cake	▶ guōbā	鍋巴

Breakfast & light meal

soybean milk	▶ dòujiāng	豆漿
baked wheat bread	▶ shāobing	燒餅
fried cruller	▶ yóutiáo	油條
steamed bread	▶ mántou	饅頭
flap jack	▶ làobǐng	烙餅
bun	▶ bāozi	包子
roasted pork bun	▶ chāshāobāo	叉燒包
steamed meat bun	▶ xiǎolóngbāo	小籠包
rice ball	▶ fàntuán	飯糰
millet congee	▶ xiǎomǐzhōu	小米粥
Cantonese congee	▶ guǎngdōngzhōu	廣東粥
wonton	▶ húntun	餛飩
boiled dumpling	▶ shuǐjiǎo	水餃
steamed dumpling	▶ zhēngjiǎo	蒸餃
pan fried dumpling	▶ guōtiē	鍋貼
meat dumpling in chili oil	▶ hóngyóu-chāoshǒu	紅油抄手
layer cake	▶ qiāncénggāo	千層糕
sweet rice cake	▶ mǐgāo	米糕

MENU

Dessert

bird's nest soup with rocksugar	▶ bīngtáng yànwō	冰糖燕窩
sweet fermented rice	▶ tiánjiǔniàng	甜酒釀
roasted sugar chestnuts	▶ tángchǎo-lìzi	糖炒栗子
almond tofu	▶ xìngrén dòufu	杏仁豆腐
red bean soup	▶ hóngdòutāng	紅豆湯
green bean soup	▶ lǜdòutāng	綠豆湯
tofu pudding	▶ dòufunǎo	豆腐腦
cotton candy	▶ miánhuātáng	棉花糖
glazed fruit kabob	▶ tánghúlu	糖葫蘆
dried persimmon	▶ shìbǐng	柿餅
sesame paste soup	▶ zhīmahú	芝麻糊
twisted stick donut	▶ máhuā	麻花

Seasoning

bean sauce	▶ dòubànjiàng	豆瓣醬
chili	▶ làjiāo	辣椒
ketchup	▶ fānqiéjiàng	番茄醬
mustard	▶ jièmojiàng	芥末醬
pepper	▶ hújiāo	胡椒
salt	▶ yán	鹽

sesame paste	▶ zhīmajiàng	芝麻醬
shacha sauce	▶ shāchájiàng	沙茶醬
soybean sauce	▶ jiàngyóu	醬油
sugar	▶ táng	糖
vinegar	▶ cù	醋

Fast Food

bread	▶ miànbāo	麵包
cake	▶ dàngāo	蛋糕
chocolate	▶ qiǎokèlì	巧克力
donut	▶ tiánmiànbāoquān	甜麵包圈
french fries	▶ zháshǔtiáo	炸薯條
fruit jelly	▶ guǒdòng	果凍
hamburger	▶ hànbǎo	漢堡
hot dog	▶ règǒu	熱狗
ice cream	▶ bīngqílín	冰淇淋
pizza	▶ báobǐng	薄餅
pudding	▶ bùdīng	布丁
salad	▶ shālā	沙拉
sandwich	▶ sānmíngzhì	三明治
toast	▶ kǎo miànbāopiàn	烤麵包片

MENU

Fruits

apple	▶ píngguǒ	蘋果
banana	▶ xiāngjiāo	香蕉
cherry	▶ yīngtáo	櫻桃
coconut	▶ yēzi	椰子
grapes	▶ pútáo	葡萄
guava	▶ bālè	芭樂
honeydew melon	▶ hāmìguā	哈密瓜
lemon	▶ níngméng	檸檬
longan	▶ lóngyǎn	龍眼
lychee	▶ lìzhī	荔枝
mango	▶ mángguǒ	芒果
orange	▶ liǔchéng	柳橙
papaya	▶ mùguā	木瓜
peach	▶ táozi	桃子
pear	▶ lí	梨
persimmon	▶ shìzi	柿子
pineapple	▶ fènglí	鳳梨
plum	▶ lǐzi	李子
starfruit	▶ yángtáo	楊桃
sugar cane	▶ gānzhè	甘蔗
tangerine	▶ júzi	橘子
watermelon	▶ xīguā	西瓜
wax apple	▶ liánwù	蓮霧

Drinks

Soft drinks

cocoa	▶ kěkě	可可
cola	▶ kělè	可樂
milk	▶ niúnǎi	牛奶
milk tea	▶ nǎichá	奶茶
mineral water	▶ kuàngquánshuǐ	礦泉水
tapioca bubble tea	▶ zhēnzhū nǎichá	珍珠奶茶
water	▶ shuǐ	水

Juice

coconut juice	▶ yēzizhī	椰子汁
guava juice	▶ bālèzhī	芭樂汁
lemonade	▶ níngméngzhī	檸檬汁
mango juice	▶ mángguǒzhī	芒果汁
mix fruit juice	▶ hùnhé guǒzhī	混合果汁
orange juice	▶ chéngzhī	橙汁
pineapple juice	▶ fènglízhī	鳳梨汁
sugar cane juice	▶ gānzhèzhī	甘蔗汁
tomato juice	▶ fānqiézhī	番茄汁
watermelon juice	▶ xīguāzhī	西瓜汁

Tea

black tea	▶ hóngchá	紅茶
Iron Goddess tea	▶ tiěguānyīn	鐵觀音
Jasmine tea	▶ mòlìhuāchá	茉莉花茶
Long Jing tea	▶ lóngjǐngchá	龍井茶
Oolong tea	▶ wūlóngchá	烏龍茶
Pu Er tea	▶ pǔ'ěrchá	普洱茶

Alcohol

beer	▶ píjiǔ	啤酒
champagne	▶ xiāngbīn	香檳
cocktail	▶ jīwěijiǔ	雞尾酒
draft beer	▶ shēngpíjiǔ	生啤酒
Kaoliang liquor	▶ gāoliángjiǔ	高粱酒
Mao Tai liquor	▶ máotáijiǔ	茅台酒
red rice wine	▶ hóngmǐjiǔ	紅米酒
red wine	▶ hóngjiǔ	紅酒
Shaoxing wine	▶ shàoxīngjiǔ	紹興酒
vodka	▶ fútèjiā	伏特加
whisky	▶ wēishìjì	威士忌
white wine	▶ báipútáojiǔ	白葡萄酒
wine	▶ pútáojiǔ	葡萄酒
Wu Chia Pee liquor	▶ wǔjiāpí	五加皮

Coffee

Blue Mountain	▶ lánshān kāfēi	藍山咖啡
Brazil Santos	▶ bāxī kāfēi	巴西咖啡
cappuccino	▶ kǎbùqínuò	卡布奇諾
decaffeinated coffee	▶ dī kāfēiyīn kāfēi	低咖啡因咖啡
hot coffee	▶ rè kāfēi	熱咖啡
iced coffee	▶ bīng kāfēi	冰咖啡
Latte	▶ nátiě kāfēi	拿鐵咖啡
Mandheling	▶ màntèníng kāfēi	曼特寧咖啡
Mocha	▶ mókǎ kāfēi	摩卡咖啡

Shopping List

Department Store

Cosmetics

cologne	▶ gǔlóngshuǐ	古龍水
eyebrow pencil	▶ méibǐ	眉筆
eye shadow	▶ yǎnyǐng	眼影
foundation	▶ fěndǐ	粉底
lip balm	▶ chúngāo ▶ hùchúngāo	唇膏 護唇膏
lipstick	▶ kǒuhóng	口紅
lotion	▶ rǔyè	乳液
mascara	▶ jiémáogāo	睫毛膏
mask	▶ miànmó	面膜
nail enamel	▶ zhǐjiayóu	指甲油
perfume	▶ xiāngshuǐ	香水
scrub cream	▶ qùjiǎozhìshuāng	去角質霜
suntan lotion	▶ fángshàiyóu	防晒油
tonic	▶ huàzhuāngshuǐ	化妝水

Jewelry & accessories

bracelet	▶ shǒuzhuó	手鐲
brooch	▶ xiōngzhēn	胸針
clock	▶ zhōng	鐘

coral	▶ shānhú	珊瑚
crystal	▶ shuǐjīng	水晶
diamond	▶ zuànshí	鑽石
earrings	▶ ěrhuán	耳環
gold	▶ huángjīn	黃金
necklace	▶ xiàngliàn	項鍊
pearl	▶ zhēnzhū	珍珠
ring	▶ jièzhi	戒指
sunglasses	▶ tàiyáng yǎnjìng	太陽眼鏡
watch	▶ biǎo	錶

Clothes

blouse	▶ nǚchènshān	女襯衫
bra	▶ xiōngzhào	胸罩
briefs	▶ nèikù	內褲
cap	▶ màozi	帽子
cardigan	▶ kāijīn máoshān	開襟毛衫
casual wear	▶ xiūxiánfú	休閒服
children's wear	▶ tóngzhuāng	童裝
coat	▶ dàyī	大衣
dress	▶ xīzhuāng ▶ yángzhuāng	西裝 洋裝
gloves	▶ shǒutào	手套

handkerchief	▶ shǒupà	手帕
jacket	▶ jiākè	夾克
jeans	▶ niúzǎikù	牛仔褲
knit shirt	▶ zhēnzhīshān	針織衫
ladies' wear	▶ nǚzhuāng	女裝
long-sleeved	▶ chángxiù	長袖
men's wear	▶ nánzhuāng	男裝
necktie	▶ lǐngdài	領帶
pajamas	▶ shuìyī	睡衣
scarf	▶ wéijīn	圍巾
shirt	▶ chènshān	襯衫
shorts	▶ duǎnkù	短褲
short-sleeved	▶ duǎnxiù	短袖
skirt	▶ qúnzi	裙子
sleeveless	▶ wúxiù	無袖
socks	▶ wàzi	襪子
sportswear	▶ yùndòngfú	運動服
stockings	▶ sīwà	絲襪
suit	▶ xīzhuāng	西裝
sweater	▶ máoyī	毛衣
swim suit	▶ yǒngzhuāng	泳裝
tops	▶ shàngyī	上衣
trousers	▶ chángkù	長褲

T-shirt	▶ T-xùshān	T 恤衫
	▶ T-xù	T 恤
turtleneck	▶ gāolǐng róngyī	高領絨衣
	▶ tàotóu shàngyī	套頭上衣
underwear	▶ nèiyī	內衣
vest	▶ bèixīn	背心
V-neck	▶ V-lǐng shàngyī	V 領上衣

Footwear

boots	▶ xuēzi	靴子
high heels	▶ gāogēnxié	高跟鞋
sandals	▶ liángxié	涼鞋
shoes	▶ xiézi	鞋子
sneakers	▶ lǚxíngxié	旅行鞋
	▶ xiūxiánxié	休閒鞋
sports shoes	▶ yùndòngxié	運動鞋

Leather goods

backpack	▶ bèibāo	背包
belt	▶ pídài	皮帶
change purse	▶ língqiánbāo	零錢包
	▶ xiǎo qiánbāo	小錢包
handbag	▶ shǒutíbāo	手提包
wallet	▶ píjiā	皮夾

Electrical goods

cellphone	▶ shǒujī	手機
digital camcorder	▶ shùmǎ shèxiàngjī ▶ shùwèi shèyǐngjī	數碼攝像機 數位攝影機
digital camera	▶ shùmǎ xiàngjī ▶ shùwèi xiàngjī	數碼相機 數位相機
electronic dictionary	▶ diànzǐ cídiǎn	電子辭典
electronic translator	▶ fānyìjī	翻譯機
household appliance	▶ jiādiàn yòngpǐn	家電用品
IC recorder	▶ lùyīnbǐ	錄音筆
laptop	▶ bǐjìběn diànnǎo ▶ bǐjìxíng diànnǎo	筆記本電腦 筆記型電腦
LED monitor	▶ yèjīng yíngmù	液晶螢幕
LED television	▶ yèjīng diànshì	液晶電視
online games	▶ xiànshàng yóuxì	線上遊戲
plasma television	▶ děnglízǐ diànshì ▶ diànjiāng diànshì	等離子電視 電漿電視
printer	▶ dǎyìnjī ▶ yìnbiǎojī	打印機 印表機
projector	▶ tóuyǐngjī	投影機
scanner	▶ sǎomiáoyí ▶ sǎomiáoqì	掃描儀 掃描器

stereo	▶ yīnxiǎng	音響
USB flash drive	▶ suíshēndié	隨身碟
video game	▶ diànzǐ yóuxì	電子遊戲
	▶ diànshì yóulèqì	電視遊樂器
video recorder	▶ lùxiàngjī	錄像機
	▶ lùyǐngjī	錄影機
Walkman	▶ suíshēntīng	隨身聽

* Throughout the region, new words, such as a PDA, MP3/MD, CD or DVD/VCD, are commonly known in English.

Supermarket

Food & drinks

alcohol	▶ lièjiǔ	烈酒
beer	▶ píjiǔ	啤酒
bread	▶ miànbāo	麵包
candy	▶ tángguǒ	糖果
canned food	▶ guàntou shípǐn	罐頭食品
coffee	▶ kāfēi	咖啡
cola	▶ kělè	可樂
cookies	▶ bǐnggān	餅乾
drinks	▶ yǐnliào	飲料
hamburger	▶ hànbǎo	漢堡

hot dog	▶ règǒu	熱狗
juice	▶ guǒzhī	果汁
lunchbox	▶ héfàn ▶ biàndāng	盒飯 便當
milk	▶ niúnǎi	牛奶
milk tea	▶ nǎichá	奶茶
mineral water	▶ kuàngquánshuǐ	礦泉水
rice wine	▶ mǐjiǔ	米酒
sandwich	▶ sānmíngzhì	三明治
seaweed	▶ hǎitái	海苔
snack	▶ língshí	零食
soda pop	▶ qìshuǐ	汽水
soybean milk	▶ dòujiāng	豆漿
sports drink	▶ yùndòng yǐnliào	運動飲料
tea	▶ chá	茶
yogurt	▶ suānnǎi ▶ yōuluòrǔ	酸奶 優酪乳

Sanitary goods

bath towel	▶ yùjīn	浴巾
conditioner	▶ rùnfàlù ▶ rùnsījīng	潤髮露 潤絲精
dental floss	▶ yáxiàn	牙線

disposable underpants	▶ miǎnxǐnèikù	免洗內褲
facial puff	▶ huàzhuāngmián	化妝棉
hair treatment	▶ hùfàrǔ	護髮乳
razor	▶ tìxūdāo ▶ guāhúdāo	剃鬚刀 刮鬍刀
sanitary napkin	▶ wèishēngjīn ▶ wèishēngmián	衛生巾 衛生棉
shampoo	▶ xǐfàlù ▶ xǐfǎjīng	洗髮露 洗髮精
shower gel	▶ mùyùlù ▶ mùyùrǔ	沐浴露 沐浴乳
soap	▶ xiāngzào	香皂
sponge	▶ hǎimián	海綿
tissue paper	▶ miànzhǐ	面紙
toilet paper	▶ wèishēngzhǐ	衛生紙
toothbrush	▶ yáshuā	牙刷
towel	▶ máojīn	毛巾

Others

bowl	▶ wǎn	碗
Chinese newspaper	▶ zhōngwénbào	中文報
chopsticks	▶ kuàizi	筷子

cup	▶ bēizi	杯子
English newspaper	▶ yīngwénbào	英文報
fork	▶ chāzi	叉子
knife	▶ xiǎodāo	小刀
paper towel	▶ zhǐjīn	紙巾
sewing kit	▶ zhēnxiànhé	針線盒
spoon	▶ tāngchí	湯匙
stamp	▶ yóupiào	郵票
stationery	▶ wénjù	文具
tape	▶ jiāodài	膠帶
water jar	▶ shuǐhú	水壺

Bookstore

book	▶ shū	書
Buddhist scripture	▶ fójīng	佛經
business management	▶ qǐyè guǎnlǐ	企業管理
classical novel	▶ gǔdiǎn xiǎoshuō	古典小說
commerce	▶ shāngyè	商業
dictionary	▶ cídiǎn	辭典
essays	▶ sǎnwén	散文

geography	▶ dìlǐ	地理
history	▶ lìshǐ	歷史
humanities & arts	▶ rénwén yìshù	人文藝術
industry	▶ gōngyè	工業
information technology	▶ zīxùn kējì	資訊科技
Lao Zi	▶ Lǎozǐ	老子
leisure life	▶ xiūxián shēnghuó	休閒生活
magazine	▶ zázhì	雜誌
medicine	▶ yīyào	醫藥
modern literature	▶ xiàndài wénxué	現代文學
philosophy	▶ zhéxué	哲學
religion	▶ zōngjiào	宗教
science	▶ kēxué	科學
The Analects of Confucius	▶ Lúnyǔ	論語
The Holy Bible	▶ Shèngjīng	聖經
Zhuang Zi	▶ Zhuāngzǐ	莊子

Audio-Visual Shop

Chinese songs	▶ zhōngwéngē	中文歌
classical music	▶ gǔdiǎn yīnyuè	古典音樂
dance music	▶ wǔqǔ	舞曲

drama	▶ xìqǔ	戲曲
electronic music	▶ diànzǐ yīnyuè	電子音樂
English songs	▶ yīngwéngē	英文歌
erhu	▶ èrhú	二胡
folk songs	▶ mínyáo	民謠
hip hop	▶ xīhāyuè	嘻哈樂
huqin	▶ húqin	胡琴
movie	▶ diànyǐng	電影
pipa	▶ pípa	琵琶
pop music	▶ liúxíng yīnyuè	流行音樂
rap	▶ ráoshéyuè	饒舌樂
traditional musical instruments	▶ chuántǒng yuèqì	傳統樂器

References

Make a Phone Call

International Dialing Codes:

Dial【IDD Prefix (International Direct Dialing)】+ 【Country Code】+【Area Code】+【User Number】

For example:

Calling from China to the U.S.

Dial【00】*1+【1】+【Area Code】+【User Number】

Calling from the U.S. to China

Dial【011】+【86】*2+【Area Code】+【User Number】

*1: Dial 002, 009, or 019 while calling from Taiwan to another country.

*2: The country code of China is 86, in Taiwan 886, and in Hong Kong 852.

Country Name	Country Code	Time Difference with China
Australia	61	0 ~ +2
Belgium	32	–7
Canada	1	–13 ~ –16
Egypt	20	–6
France	33	–7
Germany	49	–7
India	91	–2.5
Japan	81	+1
Netherlands	31	–7
New Zealand	64	+4

Portugal	351	–8
Russia	7	–5
Saudi Arabia	966	–5
South Korea	82	+1
Sweden	46	–7
U.S.A.	1	–13 ~ –16
United Kingdom	44	–8

Area Codes of Major Cities in China & Taiwan:

City Name	Characters	Area Code
In China		
Beijing	北京	10
Changchun	長春	431
Chengdu	成都	28
Chongqing	重慶	23
Dalian	大連	411
Fuzhou	福州	591
Germu	格爾木	979
Guangzhou	廣州	20
Guiyang	貴陽	851
Haerbin	哈爾濱	451
Haikou	海口	898
Hangzhou	杭州	571
Hefei	合肥	551
Huhehaote	呼和浩特	471

Jinan	濟南	531
Kunming	昆明	871
Lanzhou	蘭州	931
Nanjing	南京	25
Qiqihaer	齊齊哈爾	452
Shanghai	上海	21
Shantou	汕頭	754
Shenyang	瀋陽	24
Shenzhen	深圳	755
Shijiazhuang	石家莊	311
Suzhou	蘇州	512
Tianjin	天津	22
Wuhan	武漢	27
Xiamen	廈門	592
Xian	西安	29
Yinchuan	銀川	951

In Taiwan

Hsinchu	新竹	03
Hualien	花蓮	03
Kaohsiung	高雄	07
Taichung	台中	04
Tainan	台南	06
Taipei	台北	02
Taitung	台東	089

Climate

China has an area of 9.5 million square kilometers. Spreading over such a vast area, encompassing the various terrains, China, as you can imagine, is subject to all the extremes in weather. Generally speaking, summers are the time for rain, while winters are relatively dry.

North

Winters in the northern part of China are freezing cold, with the temperature of some areas dropping to as low as -40 ℃ (-40 ℉). During the summer, which is around May to August, daytime temperatures range from 20 ℃ to 30 ℃ (68 ℉ to 86 ℉), but still it can be bitterly cold in the night. Make sure to keep yourself warm and cozy when traveling into this area.

Central

When we talk about Central China, we are talking about the areas around *Chang Jiang* Valley, where summer means scorching heat and miserably humid condition. In some days during April and October, and especially in July and August, the temperature can surge to as high as 38 ℃ (100 ℉).

Despite the appalling heat in the summertime, you can expect wet and freezing winters. It can be as cold as in the north, although the winter is shorter.

South

The southern part of China has a fairly hot and humid summer. Summer lingers on for a stretch of more than

6 months. From April to October, the temperature can reach up to 38 ℃ (100 ℉), and it rains a lot, too. It is also the time when typhoons hit the southeast coasts.

Winter is short and relatively warm. But you want to be careful, since statistics are sometimes deceiving. Warm clothes for cold days are certainly a must.

Northwest

Moving towards the northwest, you will experience some of the most extreme terrains and weather in China. Expect scorching heat during the daytime in the desert regions. In Turpan, the temperature can rise to 47 ℃ (117 ℉).

Winters are equally unfavorable to human existence. In Urumqi, the average temperature in January is around -30 ℃ (-22 ℉).

Holidays & Festivals

Public Holidays in China:

Public Holiday	Date
New Year's Day	January 1
Chinese New Year (Spring Festival)	The 1st day of the 1st lunar month
International Women's Day	March 8
International Labor Day	May 1
Youth Day	May 4
International Children's Day	June 1
Anniversary of the founding of the Chinese Communist Party	July 1
Anniversary of the founding of the PLA	August 1
National Day	October 1

REFERENCES

The International Labor Day on the first day of May and The National Day on the first day of October are the two most important national holidays in China. They have been drawn out into weeklong holidays when city residents make a long trip to visit their relatives in the country or have a break from the tension of their daily lives. Therefore, it is not a great idea to travel into this area during these times.

Public Holidays in Taiwan:

Public Holiday	Date
New Year's Day	January 1
Chinese New Year (Spring Festival)	The 1st day of the 1st lunar month
Peace Day	February 28
Tomb-Sweeping Day	April 5
Labor Day	May 1
Dragon Boat Festival	The 5th day of the 5th lunar month
Moon Festival (Mid-Autumn Festival)	The 15th day of the 8th lunar month
National Day (Double Tenth Day)	October 10

Folk Festivals:

Spring Festival (*Chun Jie*)

Chun Jie, or the Spring Festival is in fact the traditional Chinese New Year. It falls on the 1st day of the 1st month in the Lunar Calendar.

Chun Jie ranks on top of the national festivals in terms of importance. It is the time when families reunite and have good meals together. The celebration may last for up to 15 days. According to tradition, the New Year holidays end on the first full moon, or the Lantern Festival.

Tomb-Sweeping Day (*Qingming Jie*)

On the 5th day of April, you will see many families troop off to the graveyards on the hillside on the edge

of towns. This is the day when people visit their
ancestors, cut back weeds, maintain the graves, and say
their prayers.

Dragon Boat Festival (*Duanwu Jie*)

Falling on the 5th day of the 5th month in the Lunar
Calendar, Dragon Boat Festival marks the beginning of
summer. Legend has it that *Qu Yuan*, a poet and patriot
from the Warring States Period (475-221 B.C.),
drowned himself in the river on this day. To protect his
body from being consumed by the fish, people threw
rice dumplings into the river and went out on the river
to look for his body—hence the boat race we have
today.

Ghost Festival (*Zhongyuan Jie*)

Chinese people believe that the 7th month in the Lunar
Calendar is the time when ghosts rise from the
Underworld and walk the earth, so it's not a good time
for weddings, funerals, moving house, swimming, you
name it. The 15th day of the 7th month in the Lunar
Calendar is known as *Zhongyuan Jie*. On this day,
people present their offerings to the dead, out of fear
and out of compassion at the same time.

Moon Festival/Mid-Autumn Festival (*Zhongqiu Jie*)

As indicated by its name, this festival falls in the
middle of the fall season, i.e. the 15th day of the 8th
month in the Lunar Calendar. It is the time to gaze at
the moon, eat moon cakes, and tell the romantic story of
Chang-e, a lonesome beauty now looking down from
the moon.

REFERENCES

Measurements

Temperature

To convert °C to °F, multiplied by 1.8 and add 32.
To convert °F to °C, subtract 32 and divided by 1.8.

Length, Distance & Area	multiplied by
inches to centimeters	2.54
centimeters to inches	0.39
feet to meters	0.30
meters to feet	3.28
yards to meters	0.91
meters to yards	1.09
miles to kilometers	1.61
kilometers to miles	0.62
acres to hectares	0.40
hectares to acres	2.47
Weight	**multiplied by**
ounces to grams	28.35
grams to ounces	0.035
pounds to kilograms	0.45
kilograms to pounds	2.2046
British tons to kilograms	1016
U.S. tons to kilograms	907
(In China) 斤 (jin) to grams	500
(In Taiwan) 斤 (jin) to grams	600
Volume	**multiplied by**
imperial gallons to liters	4.55
liters to imperial gallons	0.22
U.S. gallons to liters	3.79
liters to U.S. gallons	0.26

Common Measure Words

When expressing a quantity in Chinese, a measure word must follow the number and precede the noun, such as 5 běn shū (books), 3 zhī gǒu (dogs), 1 liàng chē (vehicle). Běn, zhī, and liàng are measure words that represent the nature and properties of the objects.

Measure Words	Objects Represented	Examples
ge	general use	person, bowl, apple
liàng	objects with wheels	bicycle, taxi, bus
zhāng	paper-like objects	map, ticket, pancake
běn	books, etc.	book, magazine, dictionary
zhī	animals	dog, cat, mouse
tiáo	rope-like objects	road, river, snake
jiàn	clothes	shirt, coat, jacket
shuāng	objects in pairs	a pair of hands, a pair of shoes, a pair of chopsticks
kuài	a lump of; a piece of	soap, cake, stone
bēi	a cup of; a glass of	water, coffee, beer

REFERENCES

Useful Web Sites & Telephone Numbers

Web Sites:

China Travel Net
www.ctshk.com/english/

China Tour
www.chinatour.com

Travel China Guide
www.travelchinaguide.com

Welcome to Taiwan
www.taiwan.net.tw

Travel in Taiwan
www.sinica.edu.tw/tit/

Taiwan Travel Information
www.asiatravel.com/taiwan/taiinfo.html

Telephone Numbers:

	China/Taiwan
Police	110
Fire	119
Rescue	120/119
Time Service	117
International Directory Service	115/100
Local Directory Service	114/104
Long Distance Directory Service	173/105
Weather	121/166

Mini-Dictionary

A

B

MINI-DICTIONARY

black tea hóngchá	紅茶	81	
bladder pángguāng	膀胱	265	
blanket máotǎn / tǎnzi	毛毯 / 毯子	80, 81, 104	
bleed liúxuè	流血	259, 262	
blood xuè	血	262	
blouse nǚchènshān	女襯衫	107	
blue lán	藍	167	
boarding gate dēngjīmén	登機門	83	
boarding pass dēngjīpái	登機牌	78	
boat chuán	船	85, 241	
bold stripe cū tiáowén	粗條紋	168	
bon voyage yílù-shùnfēng	一路順風	9	
bone gǔtou	骨頭	265	
bone china gǔcí	骨瓷	161	
book (n.) shū	書	181, 250	
book (v.) dìng / yùdìng	訂 / 預訂	40, 42, 78	
bookstore shūdiàn	書店	164	
born chūshēng	出生	30	
borrow jièyòng	借用	184	
bottle píng	瓶	122	
bottom dǐxia	底下	56	
boutique jīngpǐndiàn	精品店	95	
bowl wǎn	碗	117, 128	
bowling bǎolíngqiú	保齡球	236	
box hézi / xiāngzi	盒子 / 箱子	163, 176	
box office shòupiàochù	售票處	47	
boyfriend nánpéngyou	男朋友	202	
bracelet shǒuzhuó	手鐲	148	
brain nǎozi	腦子	265	
brake (n.) shāchē	煞車	276	
brand pǐnpái	品牌	160	
bread miànbāo	麵包	127	

MINI-DICTIONARY

MINI-DICTIONARY

D

E

F

MINI-DICTIONARY

gāosù gōnglù shōufèizhàn

G

H

MINI-DICTIONARY

I

J

K

knee xīgài	膝蓋	264
knife dāozi	刀子	121, 128
knock down zhuàng / zhuàngshāng	撞 / 撞傷	260, 262
know zhīdao / huì	知道 / 會	59, 121
Korean food hánguócài	韓國菜	120
Kun Opera kūnqǔ	崑曲	135

L

lacquerware qīqì	漆器	149
lamp táidēng	檯燈	102
land (v.) jiàngluò	降落	82
landscape painting shānshuǐhuà	山水畫	149
landslide tāfāng	塌方	279, 281
lane xiàngzi	巷子	53
lantern dēnglong	燈籠	149
large dàhào	大號	171
last month shàng ge yuè	上個月	25
last week shàng ge xīngqī	上個星期	26
last year qùnián	去年	24
late wǎn	晚	7
late-night show wǔyèchǎng	午夜場	231
later yíhuìr / dāihuìr	一會兒 / 待會兒	9, 33
laundry sòngxǐ yīwù	送洗衣物	106
lawyer lǜshī	律師	201
lead-free wúqiān qìyóu	無鉛汽油	73
lead the way dàilù	帶路	54
leakage lòushuǐ	漏水	277
leather pígé	皮革	161
leave líkāi	離開	30
leave a message liúhuà	留話	189
left zuǒbian	左邊	56
leg xiǎotuǐ	小腿	264

M

N

O

P

MINI-DICTIONARY

Q

R

S

T

U

V

MINI-DICTIONARY

MINI-DICTIONARY

X

Y

Z

MP3 System Requirements

Intel Pentium® compatible processors/True Color or High
Color display adapter and monitor/CD-ROM
drive/Microphone/Mouse/Speaker/Microsoft Window
Systems

MP3 Operation Procedures

1. Turn on your computer and make sure your speakers
   can run normally.
2. Place the MP3 disk in CD-ROM drive and its program
   will execute automatically.
3. If the automatic execution fails, click on "Start" button,
   select "Run" option, and type "d:\playmp3.exe" (d is
   the letter of your CD-ROM drive).